Richard Norton-Taylor

THE COLOUR OF JUSTICE

BASED ON THE TRANSCRIPTS OF

THE STEPHEN LAWRENCE INQUIRY

OBERON BOOKS
LONDON

First published in 1999 by Oberon Books Ltd
(incorporating Absolute Classics)
521 Caledonian Road, London N7 9RH
Tel: 020 7607 3637 / Fax: 020 7607 3629
e-mail: oberon.books@btinternet.com
www.oberonbooks.com

Reprinted with corrections 1999, 2004.

Cover photograph: Sean Smith, *Guardian*

Cover design: Humphrey Gudgeon

ISBN: 1 84002 107 1

Printed in Great Britain by Antony Rowe Ltd, Chippenham.

The Stephen Lawrence Trust has been registered as a charity,
is a non-sectarian, non-political, non-profit making body which
aims to help others with ambitions similar to those Stephen had
before his death, through the study of architecture and the
improvement of race relations.

Offers of help and donations shoud be made to: The Secretary,
Stephen Lawrence Trust, c/o Arthur Timothy Associates, St
John's Hall, 9 Fair Street, London, SE1 2XA

Contents

Editor's Note

THE LAWRENCE INQUIRY consisted of 69 days of public hearings. The evidence is still sinking in and continues to be debated in police circles, among lawyers, in Britain's black community, and elsewhere. Sir William Macpherson and his inquiry team published their final report in February 1999, nearly six years after Stephen Lawrence's death. Its conclusions will provoke further controversy. It may be years before its full impact can be appreciated.

The transcripts of the inquiry amount to more than eleven thousand pages, which I have distilled into about a hundred – less than one per cent. Inevitably I have had to make brutal choices about which witnesses and which exchanges to include. It has not been easy. I have not included the evidence of Detective Superintendent Ian Crampton who was in charge of the case for the first few days and took the vital decision to delay arresting five suspects. 'One of the things I have to say with hindsight,' he told the inquiry, 'is that knowing what I now know I would have arrested earlier.' He later conceded that the police had 'reasonable grounds' to arrest two days after Stephen's murder.

I have not included the evidence of Detective Superintendent Brian Weeden, who took over from Crampton. He, too, failed to arrest, suggesting at one point that he did not have the authority. Michael Mansfield QC, the Lawrence family's counsel, asked Weeden, 'Do you not find it rather disturbing that it has taken all this time for you to recognise a basic tenet of criminal law?', to which Weeden replied, 'I think it is regrettable.'

I have not included the evidence of Sir Paul Condon, the Metropolitan Police Commissioner, who apologised to Doreen and Neville Lawrence but denied that racism played a role in the investigation into Stephen's murder. He urged the inquiry not to label his force as 'institutionally racist'.

Also not included is the evidence of Imran Khan, the Lawrence family's solicitor, who did so much to bring Stephen's murder, and the police handling of the case, to public attention. Also this play does not cover the inquiry's later evidence heard outside London.

I set out to include the most telling exchanges for a theatre audience, many of whom did not hit the headlines at the time but which reflect the interlocking threads which ran throughout the inquiry – police incompetence, conscious or unconscious racism and stereotyping, and the hint of corruption in the background. And I have included exchanges which reflect the personal tensions between the police and the Lawrence family – for example, Doreen's anger when she saw Detective Chief Superintendent William Ilsley, who supervised the investigation, 'fold up' as he put it, 'screw up' as she said, a piece of paper she handed him containing the names of suspects.

Above all, I wanted to select evidence of the inquiry which presented as fair, balanced and rounded a picture as possible. It was not an easy task. But if it contributes to a greater understanding of all the issues involved, it was, I hope, worthwhile and valuable.

The Colour of Justice is the fourth of what have come to be known as The Tribunal Plays performed at the Tricycle Theatre in London. The first, in 1994, was *Half the Picture*, a dramatisation of the Scott 'arms to Iraq' inquiry, which was followed by *Nuremberg* and *Srebrenica*.

Richard Norton-Taylor
London 1999

Chronology

1993

Thursday 22 April 10:30pm
Stephen Lawrence stabbed to death.

Friday 23 April
A letter giving names of the suspects left in a phone box. Statements made to the police by various people about the attacks. 'Grant', a young man who had previously provided information, goes to the police station and accuses the Acourts of the murder.

Sunday 25 April
Neville and Doreen Lawrence approach Imran Khan to act as their solicitor.

Monday 26 April
Police surveillance of the suspects' homes begins.

Tuesday 27 April
Detective Sergeant Davidson informed that an eyewitness, 'K', had been on a bus which passed the site of the murder.

Friday 30 April
More evidence obtained that the Acourts had been near the site of the murder on the evening of 22 April.

Tuesday 4 May
Press conference held. Neville Lawrence states, 'Nothing has been done. There have been no arrests and the police won't tell us what is happening.'

Thursday 6 May
The Lawrences meet Nelson Mandela.

Friday 7 May
The Acourts and Dobson arrested and made to appear in an identity parade.

Saturday 8 May

An anti-racist march held in protest at the British National Party (BNP) bookshop in Welling.

Monday 10 May

Luke Knight arrested.

Thursday 13 May

Duwayne Brooks identifies Neil Acourt in an identity parade.

Wednesday 19 May

Interview of alleged eyewitness, 'K'.

Thursday 3 June

Duwayne Brooks identifies Luke Knight in a further identity parade.

June

After the date for the criminal proceedings is set, Stephen Lawrence's body is released and buried in Jamaica.

July

The Crown Prosecution Service (CPS) drops the prosecution. The identification evidence from Duwayne Brooks is not considered good enough to secure the conviction of Neil Acourt and Luke Knight: 'After careful consideration of the available evidence in this case, we have decided there is insufficient evidence to provide a realistic conviction.' The five suspects are discharged.

October

Duwayne arrested and charged with criminal damage and violent disorder during the protest rally at Welling held on 15 May. Detective Chief Superintendent Barker brought in to review the police investigation. The Barker Report finds that the investigation had progressed satisfactorily and that all lines of inquiry had been correctly pursued. Later, in the inquiry, he admits that he intentionally covered up any criticism of Detective Superintendent Weeden, the Senior Investigating Officer. Later in the year the inquest opens, with Michael

Mansfield QC appearing for the family. Mansfield asks for an indefinite adjournment.

1994

The renewed police investigation gives evidence to the CPS.

April

The CPS refuses to prosecute. 'Despite the police's painstaking and thorough investigation, we concluded that on the basis of the information available there is insufficient evidence to take action against any individual.'

May

Detective Superintendent Weeden, who was in charge of the investigation, meets the Lawrences for the first time. At this time the family starts to consider taking out a private prosecution, an action which is exceptionally rare. After meeting Sir Paul Condon, the Commissioner of the Metropolitan Police, and informing him that they would be pursuing the private prosecution, a second police investigation is set up, led by Detective Superintendent Mellish.

December

Duwayne appears in court charged with criminal damage and violent disorder, arising from his participation in the Welling march. According to Duwayne Brooks' lawyer's final submission to the inquiry, 'The trial judge made it clear that, because of Duwayne Brooks' trauma, any conviction would result in an absolute discharge. He invited the CPS to offer no evidence. The CPS, exceptionally, declined and persisted with the prosecution. The judge stayed the prosecution as an abuse of the process of court.'

1995

April

The private prosecution starts. Neil Acourt, Luke Knight and David Norris are arrested. Jamie Acourt is already in custody.

August

First stage of the prosecution heard at Belmarsh magistrates' court in Woolwich.

September

Neil Acourt and Luke Knight sent for trial at the Old Bailey. Doreen Lawrence makes a statement outside the court: 'No family should ever have to experience the last two years of our lives. This is the worst kind of fame. We have been brought into the public spotlight, not because of our acts but by the failure of others who were under a public duty to act. The decision of the court today stands as the first clear indictment of that failure.'

1996

April

The private prosecution heard in the the Hight Court against three of the accused. Cases against Jamie Acourt and David Norris already dropped at the committal proceedings, on the basis of poor identification evidence. The case against the other three fails when the judge rules that Duwayne Brooks' identification evidence cannot be put to the jury, because the statement from Detective Sergeant Crowley calls it into question. Crowley had accompanied Duwayne to one of the identity parades.

1997

February

The inquest is resumed, during which the five suspects refuse to answer any questions. The evidence from the police confirms the view of the Lawrences that the investigation into Stephen's murder was seriously flawed. The jury return the verdict of an unlawlful killing 'in an unprovoked racist attach by five white youths'. The Lawrences lodge a formal complaint about the behaviour of the officers on the night of the murder and subsequently, Herman Ouseley, the chair of the Commission for Racial Equality, supported by 19 Labour MPs, calls for a public inquiry.

14 February 1997, *Guardian*

A coroner's jury went beyond the bounds of their instructions to issue an extraordinary condemnation of the killers of Stephen Lawrence, the teenage victim of a racist murder. After just 30 minutes of deliberation, the jury returned a verdict of unlawful killing 'in a completely unprovoked racist attack by five white youths'.

The condemnatory words exemplified the strength of feeling the case has provoked during the Lawrence family's four-year campaign for justice. Juries are required only to return a verdict as to whether a death was unlawful, accidental or 'open'.

Doreen Lawrence, in a statement read by her sister, condemned the police handling of the initial investigation. 'The wall of silence was not only in the surrounding area where my son was killed but with police officers investigating the crime,' she said.

Mrs Lawrence described parts of the inquest as a 'circus' after watching five white youths – Neil and Jamie Acourt, David Norris, Gary Dobson and Luke Knight – all refuse to answer questions, claiming a common-law right of privelege against self-incrimination. Earlier, clearly angry and close to tears, she told the reopened inquest at Southwark coroner's court that the justice system was racist.

The family's lawyer, Imran Khan, said that the inquest confirmed to the family for the first time that there were a number of lost opportunities on the night that Stephen died as far as the police were concerned. 'The coroner has indicated that had those lost opportunities been taken up by the police there might have been a difference in what has happened over the last four years. There might have been a prosecution by the CPS.'

He said that a formal complaint would be lodged with the Police Complaints Authority against officers who were in charge of the investigations. The Metropolitan Police yesterday pledged their willingness to follow up further lines of inquiry.

…The chairman of the Commission for Racial Equality, Herman Ouseley, said important questions remained unanswered after the inquest verdict. He called for an independent inquiry to investigate 'what went wrong in the investigation of this case'.

(*Extracts written by Duncan Campbell and Alison Daniels.*)

February

Immediately after the inquest verdict, the Lawrences meet with Jack Straw, the shadow Home Secretrary.

July

Now Home Secretary, Jack Straw announces the calling of a judicial public inquiry to be chaired by Sir William Macpherson. It is scheduled to start after a Police Complaints Authority report, undertaken by the Kent Constabulary, is completed.

December

The Kent Report, as it has become known, goes to the Home Secretary. It supports the Lawrence family's claim that the police investigation was flawed, stating that there were 'significant weaknesses, omissions, and lost opportunities in the conduct of the case'.

Jane Shallice
London 1999

Where Stephen Lawrence was killed

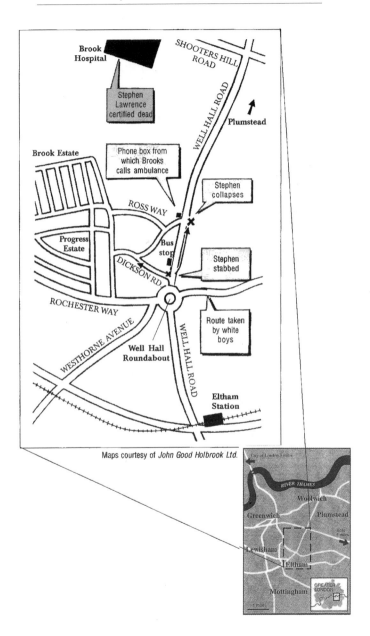

Brook Hospital

Stephen Lawrence certified dead

SHOOTERS HILL ROAD

WELL HALL ROAD

Plumstead

Brook Estate

Phone box from which Brooks calls ambulance

Stephen collapses

ROSS WAY

Progress Estate

Bus stop

Stephen stabbed

DICKSON RD

ROCHESTER WAY

WESTHORNE AVENUE

Well Hall Roundabout

WELL HALL ROAD

Route taken by white boys

Eltham Station

Maps courtesy of *John Good Holbrook Ltd.*

RIVER THAMES

Woolwich

Greenwich

Plumstead

Lewisham

Eltham

Mottingham

GREATER LONDON

The Colour of Justice was first performed at the Tricycle Theatre, London, on 6 January 1999, with the following cast:

SIR WILLIAM MACPHERSON OF CLUNY *Chairman to the inquiry*, Michael Culver

The Lawyers

EDMUND LAWSON QC *Counsel to the inquiry*, James Woolley

ANESTA WEEKES *led by Mr Lawson*, Jenny Jules

MICHAEL MANSFIELD QC *Counsel for the Lawrence family*, Jeremy Clyde

STEPHEN KAMLISH *led by Mr Mansfield*, Joseph Alessi

MARTIN SOORJOO *led by Mr Mansfield*, Ravi Aujla

MARGO BOYE-ANAWOMA *led by Mr Mansfield*, Jenny Jules

IAN MACDONALD QC *Counsel for Duwayne Brooks*, Hugh Simon

RAJIV MENON *led by Mr Macdonald*, Alex Caan

JEREMY GOMPERTZ QC *Counsel for the Commissioner of the Metropolitan Police*, Michael Stroud

SONIA WOODLEY QC *Counsel for three Superintendents*, Deborah Wilding

MICHAEL EGAN *Counsel for officers of federated rank*, Roderic Culver

The Witnesses

POLICE CONSTABLE BETHEL, Hilary Maclean

CONOR TAAFFE, Tim Woodward

POLICE CONSTABLE GLEASON, Roderic Culver

POLICE SERGEANT CLEMENT, Ken Drury

HELEN ELIZABETH AVERY, Michelle Morris

INSPECTOR GROVES, Thomas Wheatley

MR JOHN DAVIDSON *formerly Detective Sergeant*,
    William Hoyland

DETECTIVE CONSTABLE HOLDEN, Jan Chappell

DETECTIVE INSPECTOR BULLOCK, Ken Drury

MR WILLIAM ILSLEY *formerly Detective Chief
    Superintendent*, Mark Penfold

WILLIAM JAMES MELLISH *formerly Detective Superintendent*,
    Michael Attwell

IAN JOHNSTON *Assistant Commissioner Metropolitan Police*,
    Tim Woodward

JAMIE ACOURT, Christopher Fox

HOWARD YOUNGERWOOD *Crown Prosecutioner*,
    Thomas Wheatley

MR NEVILLE LAWRENCE, Tyrone De Rizzio

MRS DOREEN LAWRENCE, Yvonne Pascal

DUWAYNE BROOKS, Leon Stewart

GRACE VAUGHAN *Computer operator*, Nalina Tobierre

STEPHEN WELLS *Secretary to the inquiry*,
    Martin Newcombe

Court stenographer and others played by the company.

Director, Nicolas Kent, with Susan Fletcher-Jones

Designer, Bunny Christie

Costumes, Heather Leat

Lighting, Chris Davey

Production Manager, Shaz McGhee

The play transferred to the Victoria Palace in the West End on
3 March 1999, and for that production the part of Howard
Youngerwood was deleted, and Stephen Kamlish was played
by Paul Mari, Conor Taaffe by Michael Cochrane and Ian
Johnston by Thomas Wheatley.

Opening statements by Macpherson of Cluny, Edmund Lawson QC, Michael Mansfield QC and Jeremy Gompertz QC

MACPHERSON: The procedure of the hearings will be reasonably informal: nobody need stand to ask questions unless they wish to do so. And of course people may come and go exactly as they please.

Inevitably this room looks rather like a court, but the stricter rules of procedure and evidence do not apply to us in our search for the truth.

Our hope is that, at the end of the day, we will establish what happened and what may have gone wrong over these last years in connection with the investigation and management of this case.

To Mr and Mrs Lawrence, these years must have been dreadful. We hope sincerely that while nothing can alleviate the pain and loss which they have suffered, they may accept that all of us have done our best to establish what was done so that the future may not see repetition of any errors which may be uncovered during our hearings.

We will now turn to Mr Edmund Lawson, Queen's Counsel.

LAWSON: Stephen Lawrence was brutally murdered. The attack upon him was obviously cowardly, was unprovoked and was demonstrably racist. He was attacked in the street. He was black. His attackers were white.

No-one has been convicted for his murder. It might be appropriate just to remind the Inquiry and to inform those who listen of this description of him by someone who knew him at the Cambridge Harriers Athletic Club of which he was an active and successful member. Quite coincidently the someone was a policeman who knew him at the club because his son was involved. "During the period I knew Stephen," he said, "I never saw him display any form of aggression and would describe his temperament as the same as his father – quiet and unassuming, exemplary character." He was a young man who had never come into contact with, or the notice of, the police.

It appears that in a number of very material respects the police conduct of the investigation went badly wrong, not least in the decision to delay arrests of the principle suspects who were identified from various sources immediately after the murder. We will be inviting you to consider, and producing evidence to assist you to answer the question: were any of the errors due to simple, or perhaps more accurately, gross incompetence, or were they as some vociferously asserted – and as police officers have vigorously denied – attributable to or contributed to directly or indirectly by racism?

Nobody, police or civilian, has any proper basis for declining to assist this inquiry in its quest for the truth and that includes those who I will be referring to as the five suspects: Neil and Jamie Acourt, Norris, Dobson and Knight.

Neither Stephen Lawrence nor Duwayne Brooks did anything to provoke an argument, let alone a fight. They moved away a little from the bus stop looking to see if there was a bus coming when a group of some five or six white youths approached them. Duwayne Brooks recounted that he heard at least one of them make a reference to "nigger". He shouted to his friend to run, but Stephen could not because he was surrounded by thugs, attacked by one or more of them and knocked to the ground.

The first issue to be considered relates to first aid. It appears from the evidence that no police officer sought to administer first aid.

It seems, as a matter of tragic fact, that Stephen's injuries were so severe that first aid would not, in any event, have helped him. But questions do arise – whether first aid was denied by the police because "they did not want to dirty their hands with a black man's blood", as Mrs Lawrence asked after the inquest into her son's death. A witness on the night told her that Jamie and Neil Acourt were walking around the corner. Apparently one of the Acourt brothers carries a machete down his right hand trouser leg.

That information came to the police on the 24th of April. Apparently no action was taken until a week later.

On the 13th of May, Mr Brooks did identify Neil Acourt. On the 3rd of June, he identified Knight on another parade. The identifications led to each of those two men being charged with the murder of Stephen Lawrence. Unfortunately, a Sergeant Crowley asserts that at the time of the parade when Knight was identified, Mr Brooks made some comments to him suggesting that he had received information before the parade which may have enabled him to make the identification or prompted him as to who to identify.

Mr Brooks disputed Crowley's account. The importance of it is obvious. Mr Brooks' identification of those suspects was vital. The private prosecution that followed much later was forced, in effect, to be abandoned once Mr Brooks' evidence was excluded by the judge.

On the evening of the 23rd of April, there first came on the scene a man who has been given the name "Grant".

He accused the Acourts and Norris of Stephen Lawrence's murder.

The message stated: "The Acourt brothers call themselves the Krays. In fact, you can only join the gang if you stab someone."

Some of the suspects were under surveillance from the 26th of April. What was the object of this surveillance operation? There was a particularly crass failure. A photographer was put in place to keep surveillance on the Acourts. Before he got his camera set up, he saw somebody leaving their house with what appeared to be clothing in a bin bag, get into a car and clear off. He made no report at the time of either of these events.

This was a racist murder, there is no doubt about that. It was recognised as such by the police. I am bound to say that it is repellant that anybody who commits a murder should get away with it and anyone who does so and murders for racist motives and should escape is doubly repellant.

MANSFIELD: The magnitude of the failure in this case, we say, cannot be explained by mere incompetence or a lack of direction by senior officers or a lack of execution and application by junior officers, nor by woeful under-resourcing. So much was missed by so many that deeper causes and forces must be considered.

We suggest these forces relate to two main propositions. The first is that the victim was black and racism, both conscious and unconscious, permeated the investigation. Secondly, the fact that the perpetrators were white and were expecting some form of protection.

The fact that the same teenagers are equally capable of killing or maiming anyone in their way does not preclude them from being racist; racists rarely concentrate their venom on the black population or the

Jewish population or whoever happens to be the ethnic group which they regard as barely worth living. When Doreen Lawrence first left home after this appalling crime, merely to go shopping locally, in a car park she was confronted by a woman who indicated that her son would not have been killed if he had not been there.

It went on, this racist force. Their tyres have been slashed, their home has been watched by white youths and barely two weeks ago, the memorial plaque was desecrated, painted, daubed, and smashed with a hammer. These are activities that the Jewish population are only too familiar with. It was on the spot where Stephen died.

GOMPERTZ: Sir, it is a matter of the greatest regret to the Commissioner and to the Metropolitan Police Service that no one has been successfully prosecuted for the callous murder of Stephen Lawrence.

With hindsight, the Metropolitan Police Service acknowledges that it should have done better. The Metropolitan Police are determined to learn every possible lesson from any constructive criticism which emerges from this inquiry.

Although it is right and proper that their actions and attitudes should be closely scrutinised, the broad allegations of racism are unfair to all of those officers to whom many people owe a great debt of gratitude. Stephen's murder was a callous, evil, act committed by callous, evil, people. It is they and they alone who should bear the guilt for ending such a promising and optimistic young life.

From the evidence of Police Constable Bethel, 25 March 1998

LAWSON: I propose to call the first witnesses who attended the scene. The first two on-duty officers were Mr

Gleason and Miss Bethel. I am going to call Bethel first because she has a pressing engagement.

MACPHERSON: Yes.

LAWSON: Can I ask her to come in, come to the witness box and perhaps be sworn.

BETHEL: I do solemnly, sincerely and truly declare and affirm that the evidence I shall give shall be the truth, the whole truth and nothing but the truth.

MACPHERSON: Do be seated please. I do not think there is any need for any witness to talk, so to speak, at the microphone. They are very sensitive.

LAWSON: Your name, I think, is Linda Jane Bethel, is it not?

BETHEL: That's correct, sir.

LAWSON: Is it Miss or Mrs?

BETHEL: Mrs.

LAWSON: The first of the identified issues, which is principally concerned with the first aid given or not given at the scene. By way of background, it might, I think, be helpful if I were to just briefly divert to the chronology. You do not have this in front of you – Mrs Bethel just bear with me if you will – but, as we can see, this refers to some events that occurred during the evening of Thursday, the 22nd of April 1993 when Stephen Lawrence and Duwayne Brooks were out together. It deals at the bottom of the second page in very brief terms with the incident and the attack upon Stephen Lawrence is timed at around 10.40. A 999 call; you can see the timing of it: 22.44 on that evening. The location is given, the number of the phone box that was used.

And the message is: "Assaulted with an iron bar" and the name of Mr Brooks is given.

That night, Thursday, the 22nd of April, you were on duty with Constable Gleason, is that right?

BETHEL: That's correct.

LAWSON: When you got the call, the information you were given – there had been a suspected use of an iron bar, is that right?

BETHEL: That's correct.

LAWSON: There were no difficulties as far as you were concerned in seeing the blood coming from his body?

BETHEL: No, not at all.

LAWSON: When you saw the large amount of blood, you immediately called your control room asking them to hurry up the ambulance?

BETHEL: Yes, that's correct.

LAWSON: Did you have a first-aid kit in your police car?

BETHEL: To the best of my knowledge, yes.

LAWSON: Was it ever taken out of the car that night?

BETHEL: No.

LAWSON: Do you know the reason for that?

BETHEL: It wasn't deemed that we could actually use the first aid kit to any great benefit.

LAWSON: What would your training indicate to you should be done if you came across somebody who has apparently suffered a wound from which he is losing a lot of blood?

BETHEL: We were told that Stephen had a head wound. He was in the recovery position when we arrived. There was no obvious wound to see where the blood was coming from. We believed an ambulance would be there within minutes.

LAWSON: You have indicated that your attention was drawn to Duwayne Brooks, as you now know him to be?

BETHEL: Yes, that is correct.

LAWSON: You said he was walking around the scene very distressed?

BETHEL: Yes.

LAWSON: You asked what happened, who had done this? And he said: "A group of six white men."

BETHEL: Yes.

LAWSON: Then afterwards saying: "Where is the fucking ambulance? I didn't call the police"?

BETHEL: That's right.

LAWSON: You told him the ambulance was coming. You said you tried to get him to explain what happened but he was very excitable and upset and all he could tell you was that he had told his friend Stephen to run with him away from the youths.

BETHEL: That's correct.

LAWSON: You sent other officers who arrived off to search for the suspects; is that correct?

BETHEL: Yes, that's correct.

LAWSON: You did say: "I did try to find a pulse." How did you seek to check his pulse?

BETHEL: I believe I would have put my fingers to his neck.

LAWSON: Can you explain why you say, "I believe"?

BETHEL: The main reason being I think having dealt with Duwayne for quite a while beforehand it was obviously quite a hyped-up situation and in retrospect it is quite likely I felt my own pulse.

LAWSON: Mr Taaffe says: "At no point when I was at the scene do I recall anybody establishing that Stephen's injuries were stab wounds." You would not disagree with that?

BETHEL: No, no.

LAWSON: Still you didn't know it was stabbing?

BETHEL: No.

LAWSON: The suggestion that has been made publicly is that perhaps an explanation for the lack of first-aid attention was "police officers not wishing to dirty their hands with a black man's blood". Tell us your feelings about that.

BETHEL: I don't see myself as a racist. I don't think I act in a racist manner. I don't believe I am racist.

LAWSON: That is all I want to ask you. Thank you very much.

KAMLISH: I am going to deal with this witness. Can I do it sitting down? I am Stephen Kamlish. I am acting for the Lawrence family. Can I ask you about your first aid training? You do accept, do you not, that one of the most important matters for a person with a first-aid qualification attending a bleeding person is to try and staunch the blood?

BETHEL: If we hadn't been told it was a head injury, then perhaps I would have started searching through his clothing. It was dark.
I believed the best thing to do for Stephen was to leave him where he was.

KAMLISH: Why is the fact that it was dark relevant?

BETHEL: Because I couldn't see where any blood was coming from; it wasn't obvious.

KAMLISH: You had a torch in your car?

BETHEL: Yes.

KAMLISH: That was parked a few feet away?

BETHEL: Yes.

KAMLISH: Did you go and get the torch?

BETHEL: No.

KAMLISH: Did you ask somebody else to get the torch?

BETHEL: No.

KAMLISH: Why not?

BETHEL: I don't know.

KAMLISH: Nobody mentioned the word "stabbing" at the scene?

BETHEL: No.

KAMLISH: Were you concerned that you had not in fact looked for the injury?

BETHEL: Obviously, because of the amount of upset it has caused and the amount of attention there has been on it, yes. I do now regret that I didn't look at the injury.

KAMLISH: It is fair to say, is it not, that no one while you were there tried to identify the wound?

BETHEL: Not that I saw.

KAMLISH: No police officer?

BETHEL: Not that I saw, no.

KAMLISH: Is it fair to say that once you saw the fact that Stephen's chest was drenched in blood, coupled with his unconsciousness and the fact you believed he had a head injury, you must have by then felt that his injury was life-threatening?

BETHEL: I appreciated it was much more serious than I anticipated. I hadn't assumed it was life threatening. I hadn't assumed he was going to die.

KAMLISH: You went back to the hospital the next day to speak to the sister who cared for him?

BETHEL: It was because we were upset and we wanted to talk about it with somebody who obviously knew exactly what had happened.

KAMLISH: One of the reasons you went back was wondering whether you could have done more?

BETHEL: Mmm.

KAMLISH: Yes?

BETHEL: Yes. And she said no.

KAMLISH: In view of the questions I have asked you and the answers you have given about your failure to touch Stephen, can I just ask you some questions on another connected topic. Do you have any experience of equal opportunities or race-awareness training?

BETHEL: I believe we had training at Hendon.

KAMLISH: What ways do you consider in this country racism manifests itself?

BETHEL: Obviously in all sorts of ways…

MACPHERSON: I do not think that as broad a question as that is probably appropriate, Mr Kamlish.

KAMLISH: Perhaps these questions will relate to other officers. Perhaps I will ask a more focused question, dealing with your personal experience. Have you ever been present when someone has suffered racism in whatever form?

BETHEL: No.

KAMLISH: Never?

BETHEL: No.

KAMLISH: Never heard a racist comment in the Metropolitan Police by any police officer?

BETHEL: I'm aware that comments are made and, yes, they are heard, but I can't specifically recall any. I am not saying it doesn't exist.

KAMLISH: Thank you.

GOMPERTZ: Would you have behaved in exactly the same way if the victim had been white?

BETHEL: Yes.

GOMPERTZ: Can I ask you, please, to look at your interview? Perhaps it can be put on the screen. I hope we will find it at PCA (Police Complaints Authority) 48, pages 239 and 240. Can you look, please, at the next page, because you are asked there, just towards the bottom of the part that is on the screen now: "What is your stance on racism?" You answer: "It is despicable. There is absolutely no need for it whatsoever. I don't understand why it exists and why people have a problem with other people." Does that accurately summarise your feeling about racism?

BETHEL: Yes.

GOMPERTZ: Thank you very much.

MACDONALD: Mrs Bethel, can I say that I represent Duwayne Brooks. When you arrived, there is absolutely no dispute about this, it must have been quite clear to you that Duwayne Brooks was clearly very distressed?

BETHEL: Oh yes.

MACDONALD: Duwayne Brooks told you that the incident had started off when one of the white boys had said words to the effect: "What, what, nigger?"

BETHEL: I don't doubt he said that. I can't remember. I'm sure he did.

MACDONALD: Do you remember him saying something like this: "I fucking told you where they went. Are you deaf? Why don't you go and look for them?"

BETHEL: I certainly don't remember it, but there were an awful lot of aggressive swearing comments made. He could well have said that.

MACDONALD: Or something like it. It was in that context, I suggest, that he asked you if you could not take his friend in the police car to the hospital?

BETHEL: Again, I don't remember that being asked. It might well have been, I don't know.

MACDONALD: Is it within your police experience that you stopped someone like Duwayne in the street, or driving a car, or whatever it is, and when you stop them they get mad at you, they swear at you, they call you names and maybe end up assaulting you?

BETHEL: It is my experience with some people that you can end up getting that reaction.

MACDONALD: Is that something from your police experience that you would find when you are dealing with young black men?

BETHEL: No, I am saying generally.

MACDONALD: It is not something, is it, you are likely to experience with little old ladies?

BETHEL: No, but generally speaking it can happen. I mean, I have had a little old lady try and bite me.

MACDONALD: Your reaction to seeing Duwayne in the state that you have described is that you understand now that he was traumatised by the event that had taken place?

BETHEL: At the time I was a police officer there with him and he was, you know… He hated my guts.

From the evidence of Conor Andrew Taaffe, 26 March 1998

MACPHERSON: Thank you very much for coming. Mr Taaffe, you have been involved in giving evidence so much that I understand that your personal life has been disrupted.

LAWSON: Your name is Conor Andrew Taafe, is it not?

TAAFFE: That's right, yes.

LAWSON: You and your wife had gone to a prayer meeting at the local Catholic church?

TAAFFE: Correct.

LAWSON: You left about 10.35 and started to walk down towards the Well Hall roundabout. Is that right?

TAAFFE: That's correct, yes. Mmm.

LAWSON: Then there came to your notice a couple of young black boys who were jogging along?

TAAFFE: Yes.

LAWSON: As you thought at first, jogging?

TAAFFE: Yes, yes.

LAWSON: Of course, you know now they were not jogging, or simply jogging. Now you appreciate that one of them, the one in front, was Duwayne Brooks?

TAAFFE: Yes.

LAWSON: And the one behind was Stephen Lawrence?

TAAFFE: Mmm. When I say jogging, I didn't so much mean that I thought they were out jogging for exercise, just to sort of describe the pace. They seemed to be running. I did sense immediately something wrong, something dangerous, something suspicious straight away. It just – you just knew, you know.

LAWSON: You saw Stephen, to use your words, "crash onto the pavement", is that right?

TAAFFE: Mmm.

LAWSON: In your statement, you describe noticing at first Duwayne Brooks who was standing in the middle of the road?

TAAFFE: Yes.

LAWSON: And he appeared to be trying to flag down passing cars?

TAAFFE: He was, yes.

LAWSON: Once you had appreciated, and very quickly you did, as your wife had said, that this was something serious, you went straight over towards where Stephen had fallen, did you not?

TAAFFE: Yes, yes.

LAWSON: You went and bent down by Stephen; is that right?

TAAFFE: That's right, yes. He was definitely still alive at that stage.

LAWSON: You carried on holding Stephen's head with your hand on his back?

TAAFFE: Mmm.

LAWSON: And I think you were praying over him?

TAAFFE: Yes.

LAWSON: Then the first police car arrived?

TAAFFE: Mmm, yeah.

LAWSON: That as we know had a woman and a male police officer?

TAAFFE: Yes, yes.

LAWSON: Did the woman police officer pay any attention to Stephen as opposed to asking you what happened?

TAAFFE: She immediately came to his head.

LAWSON: She put a finger to the front of his mouth?

TAAFFE: Yes.

LAWSON: She said she thought there was some breathing?

TAAFFE: Yes, that's right.

LAWSON: You tried and felt nothing?

TAAFFE: Yes.

LAWSON: Did you see her take or feel for a pulse?

TAAFFE: I don't think so. I don't think so.

LAWSON: At the scene at that time did you have any inkling he was suffering from stab wounds? Did anyone say anything about that?

TAAFFE: I don't recall anyone mentioning stab wounds.

LAWSON: I am grateful to you. Would you wait there please.

KAMLISH: Mr Taaffe, when you first saw Stephen and Duwayne you saw Stephen holding his upper chest?

TAAFFE: Yes.

KAMLISH: The blood you saw was clearly coming from the upper body?

TAAFFE: Yes.

KAMLISH: There could not have been any doubt in the WPC's mind, could there, that this was extremely serious; that this was either life-threatening or his life was extinct?

TAAFFE: I think she was aware this was a very serious situation and that, therefore, her response to it was to get things happening: get an ambulance, find out what had happened. Do you know what I mean? I suppose she is a police officer, not a first aider, doctor, surgeon, paramedic.

KAMLISH: She is in fact first-aid trained.

TAAFFE: Oh, right. Oh, right.

KAMLISH: Your wife cradled Stephen's head at some point?

TAAFFE: Yes, yes, and she spoke in his ear. I thought it was such a lovely thing for her to say because Louise and I both knew that hearing is one of the last things to go, and so, while he was there, she said: "You are loved. You are loved." I had some blood on my hands. When I went home – this isn't material, but I will say it anyway – I went home and washed the blood off my hands with some water in a container, and there is a rose bush in our back garden, a very, very old, huge rose bush – rose tree is I suppose more appropriate – and I poured the water with his blood in it into the bottom of that rose tree. So in a way I suppose he is kind of living on a bit.

MACPHERSON: From the moment he fell into the position you have described, Stephen was not moved by anyone at all?

TAAFFE: No, no.

MACPHERSON: Yes, Mr Gompertz.

GOMPERTZ: You have said that when the WPC arrived, she crouched down?

TAAFFE: Yes, yes.

GOMPERTZ: So whether she did the right thing or the wrong thing, she was certainly being attentive to Stephen?

TAAFFE: Absolutely, yes. I wasn't aware that the WPC was a first aider. But having said that I wonder what difference it would have made. I mean, if someone stabs you and punctures an artery close to your heart even if a surgeon had been on the scene, he wouldn't have had the equipment. What could you do?

MACDONALD: Mr Taafe, I think we all appreciate that you did a wonderful thing that night. I just wanted to ask about the moment before you crossed the road, you had some fears about what was happening? You sensed danger.

TAAFFE: Yes, yes. I sensed that something was amiss, something suspicious, something dangerous. Perhaps they were running away from somewhere, perhaps they had been involved in a violent fight, you know.

MACDONALD: You have two young black men running along the road?

TAAFFE: Yes.

MACDONALD: You thought they might be about to commit a mugging or something like that?

TAAFFE: The thought flashed through my mind, being wary of the situation, that perhaps it was a ploy. One would fall down and you would think: "Oh my God, there's something wrong." You would go over and the other might get you. That did pass through my mind.

MACDONALD: Was that because it was two young black men running along the other side of the road?

TAAFFE: I would say that that was part of my assessment, yes.

From the evidence of Police Constable Gleason, 26 March 1998

MACPHERSON: Mr Gleason, will you sit to give your evidence and Mr Lawson, counsel to the inquiry, will start.

LAWSON: Thank you, sir. For everybody's information, the primary sources of evidence for this witness, is his temporary statement, PCA 38, and extensive interviews with the Kent Constabulary.

Constable Gleason, we are told you have had first-aid training?

GLEASON: Yes, sir.

LAWSON: You went to the hospital, yes, escorting the ambulance?

GLEASON: That's correct sir, yes.

LAWSON: Do you have any training, Mr Gleason, as to how you should deal with bereaved relatives?

GLEASON: No specific training, no, sir.

LAWSON: You will appreciate, of course, the trauma, the distress such people would feel?

GLEASON: Yes.

LAWSON: And the need for information?

GLEASON: Yes.

LAWSON: What did you do about that to comfort them or to give them information at the hospital?

GLEASON: As far as I recall I can remember speaking to Mr Lawrence outside the resuscitation room. What the context of that conversation was, I am afraid I just cannot remember.

LAWSON: So you had some conversation with him?

GLEASON: Yes, I did.

LAWSON: Did you have any sort of conversation with Mrs Lawrence?

GLEASON: No, I didn't.

LAWSON: At no stage?

GLEASON: At no stage, no.

LAWSON: With hindsight, PC Gleason, do you not think you should have made an effort?

GLEASON: I believe I did make an effort on the night, sir.

LAWSON: Make an effort to speak with Mrs Lawrence, speak with the family?

GLEASON: I can remember Mrs Lawrence was very, very, upset. Understandably so. I spoke to Mr Lawrence and I can also remember speaking to other members of the family as they left the hospital later in the morning.

LAWSON: You also spoke to Duwayne Brooks, did you not?

GLEASON: I did speak to Duwayne Brooks, yes.

LAWSON: You described his excitable state at the scene. What was his state at the hospital?

GLEASON: At first he was still excitable until I actually managed to calm him down and take the necessary information that is in my pocket book.

LAWSON: You better tell us about the information you got from him. For these purposes can we have on the screen PCA 45 at page 72. This is your handwriting, is it not?

GLEASON: Yes.

MACPHERSON: Do you want the witness to read it?

LAWSON: It would be quicker.

GLEASON: (*Reads.*) "We got on a 286 bus at Eltham bus station. We got off at Well Hall roundabout. We waited until 10.40 pm and we walked slowly down to the roundabout and I saw about six white boys coming up Well Hall Road on the other side of the road.

"I said to Steve that there was a bus coming. Steve was about ten yards from me. I saw the youths cross the road towards Stephen. I said to Stephen: 'See the bus.' One of the youths who had blue jeans, his hair was bushy, light brown and stuck out, he was about nineteen or twenty, he said: 'What, what, nigger?' I knew they were coming for us and I shouted: 'Steve, run.' I ran but I then turned back to see if Stephen was running. I saw the same youth who was in front of Stephen strike down with one of his arms on Stephen's head, I think.

"Stephen fell to the floor and I ran back towards him. The youths ran off and Stephen got up and ran across the road. I was telling him to run. He said: "Look at me, what is wrong?' I could see blood trickling down his chest. He then just fell. Before striking Stephen I saw the youth pull something from his jacket. It could have been a wood or metal bar."

LAWSON: Thank you. Then the next note, you say: "I was present when Mr Neville Lawrence identified the body of his son at the Brook hospital in the resuscitation room one."

GLEASON: Yes.

LAWSON: You appreciated the seriousness of the stab wounds only really at the hospital. Is that right?

GLEASON: That is when I realised he had been stabbed, yes.

LAWSON: Did you understand, as some others did, that he had been hit on the head with an iron bar?

GLEASON: That was the information that first came out: "Hit over the head with an iron bar."

LAWSON: Which, if your evidence of your examination is true, you quickly realised was wrong information?

GLEASON: I could not see any wound to the head.

THE COLOUR OF JUSTICE

LAWSON: Thank you.

MACPHERSON: Yes, Mr Kamlish.

KAMLISH: You did not find anything on the head. You saw the blood coming from elsewhere. That is right, is it not?

GLEASON: I didn't know where the blood was coming from.

KAMLISH: It is the most obvious thing at the time, is it not, that he might have been stabbed?

GLEASON: Well, it wasn't obvious to me, no, sir.

KAMLISH: Why did you not move him slightly to see if there was a wound, such as a chest wound, which you could staunch the flow of blood from?

GLEASON: Because I didn't want to move him.

KAMLISH: Why?

GLEASON: Because an ambulance was on its way and I felt that he was best left in the position he was in.

KAMLISH: What, to bleed to death, as we now know happened?

GLEASON: I didn't know he was going to bleed to death.

KAMLISH: He was unconscious, was he not?

GLEASON: Yes, he was.

KAMLISH: You say you checked his pulse?

GLEASON: Yes, sir.

KAMLISH: Where did you check it?

GLEASON: On the wrist.

KAMLISH: Which wrist?

GLEASON: I cannot remember, sir.

KAMLISH: You really cannot remember all of this?

GLEASON: No, sir, it is a long time ago.

KAMLISH: It is a long time ago, but it is probably one of the most significant events in your life, is it not?

GLEASON: Yes, sir.

KAMLISH: You went to the hospital. Why did you decide that Mr Lawrence was the person you should take to the identification?

GLEASON: He appeared to be very calm.

KAMLISH: Very calm?

GLEASON: Yes.

KAMLISH: I see. Did you ask him whether he would mind doing it?

GLEASON: I honestly do not remember.

KAMLISH: What was said about the identification; do you remember any of the words at all?

GLEASON: I am afraid I cannot say what the words were.

KAMLISH: You see, Mr Gleason, the family had been in to identify Stephen about half an hour before. So if you are telling the truth, this would be a completely unnecessary event?

GLEASON: I am not aware of that.

KAMLISH: You are aware, are you not, that not a single member of the hospital staff recalls this event, your going in with Mr Lawrence to identify the body. You know that?

GLEASON: No, I don't, but it is noted in my pocket book that this has happened.

KAMLISH: Did you ask him to sign your pocket book to confirm that he had made the identification?

GLEASON: No, I didn't.

KAMLISH: Why not?

GLEASON: I felt it was traumatic enough to see his son there. There was no way I was going to thrust a pocket book on to him and say, please sign here for this identification.

KAMLISH: Do you know why, in the light of what you just said, the family were taken formally to identify their son on Saturday at the mortuary?

GLEASON: No, I don't, sir.

KAMLISH: Just describe what happened when you got into the resus room, please?

GLEASON: Mr Lawrence identified his son.

KAMLISH: Who went where and who did what?

GLEASON: I don't remember where we stood.

KAMLISH: Come on, Mr Gleason, what was Mr Lawrence's reaction?

GLEASON: Distressed, shocked.

KAMLISH: Did he cry?

GLEASON: I honestly cannot remember.

KAMLISH: Did he touch his son's body?

GLEASON: I don't know. I cannot remember.

KAMLISH: This did not happen, did it?

GLEASON: Well, it did happen because it is noted in my pocket book.

KAMLISH: With Stephen still there?

GLEASON: Yes.

KAMLISH: So you wrote your witness statement in the resuscitation room with no-one else in there except Stephen's lifeless body?

GLEASON: I believe WPC Bethel came up at some point but it was just myself and Stephen.

KAMLISH: You say that you radioed Duwayne Brooks' account?

GLEASON: It was radioed out what he said, yes, whether they recorded it, I don't know.

KAMLISH: They would have to receive it, would they not?

GLEASON: Everyone would receive it in that area.

KAMLISH: Exactly. It is probably the most crucial information that the Metropolitan Police Service would have received that night at that early stage, a description of the suspects?

GLEASON: Yes.

KAMLISH: There is no recording of this radio message, you know that, do you not?

GLEASON: No, I don't.

KAMLISH: May I ask you briefly about your experience of racism? Have you experienced racism in the police force?

GLEASON: I have probably been present when comments have been made.

KAMLISH: By other police officers?

GLEASON: By other people in general. I can't recollect…

KAMLISH: Other police officers?

GLEASON: I'm sorry, I cannot remember any specific racist remarks being made by police officers.

KAMLISH: How long have you been a police officer, I am sorry?

GLEASON: Fourteen years.

KAMLISH: And you have never heard a police officer make a racist remark?

GLEASON: I cannot remember a police officer making a racist remark. I am not denying that may ever happen.

MACPHERSON: Mr Gleason, you were actually the only police officer who was at the hospital more or less throughout, were you not, from the time that Stephen was taken there until you left at four o'clock in the morning?

GLEASON: That's correct, sir, yes.

MACPHERSON: I think I have to say this, that it looks to me very much as if the liaison with the family was hopeless because they feel very much that no attention was paid to them at all. You understand what I mean, do you not? You may have done your best in what you say you did, but who would have been responsible for sending somebody to do that job specifically? Who was your boss, so to speak?

GLEASON: Who was actually overall in command of the incident I don't know.

From the evidence of Sergeant Clement, 27 March 1998

LAWSON: On that particular night, the night we are looking at, you with other officers were on board what I think are called a group carrier?

CLEMENT: Yes, that's correct.

LAWSON: Roughly how many of you would there be and of what rank?

CLEMENT: Possibly an inspector, sergeant and six PCs on each vehicle and the inspector... (*Inaudible.*) ...all three vehicles.

LAWSON: You let your voice drop occasionally. Was the inspector with you that night?

CLEMENT: Yes.

LAWSON: Is that Inspector Groves?

CLEMENT: Inspector Groves, yes.

LAWSON: You were called to the scene of what we know now to be Stephen Lawrence's murder?

CLEMENT: We responded to a call, to an emergency call there and chose to accept the call and went there.

LAWSON: Do you have any notes, Sergeant Clement, of the incident?

CLEMENT: I do not.

LAWSON: I wonder if we could look, please, at the screen, PCA 38 page 228. This is a printed, or typed, version of your witness statement made on the 1st of May 1993. Do you see that?

CLEMENT: I can see the statement. I can't see the date. I have got the date now, yes.

LAWSON: These computer print things are not easy to read sometimes. I am going to ask you to have a look at this. You described there responding to a call that related to an assault with an iron bar?

CLEMENT: Yes.

LAWSON: You then say: "We began to search the vicinity for a group of six males concerned"?

CLEMENT: That's correct.

LAWSON: On your arrival, you searched the vicinity. Where did you search, can you remember, on your first search?

CLEMENT: The first search we did, that was in our carrier – a mobile search – would have been the streets along Downman Road, Phineas Pett Road, the general side streets around there and back to the roundabout, from what I can recall, and past where Stephen was laying up to the Welcome Inn.

LAWSON: You then said in your statement: "You gave directions for a sweeping search"?

CLEMENT: Yes.

LAWSON: It does not seem at the time you made this statement that Dickson Road meant anything in particular to you. Is that a fair comment?

CLEMENT: Yeah, we knew of Dickson Road because we searched that Dickson Road, because the suspects had made off down Dickson Road.

LAWSON: You moved down Dickson Road searching for any kind of weapon?

CLEMENT: Anything really. Evidence, maybe a jacket discarded, anything.

LAWSON: Is this your entire team, so to speak?

CLEMENT: Yes, probably half a dozen to a dozen officers.

LAWSON: What were their instructions?

CLEMENT: We searched the gardens…

LAWSON: Forgive me, what were they being told to look for?

CLEMENT: The original call was of a male being attacked by an iron bar.

LAWSON: Anyone told you different before you went off on your search?

CLEMENT: I can't remember.

LAWSON: Did you have any artificial lighting, torches or anything of that sort with you?

CLEMENT: We had a rechargeable torch about that size.

LAWSON: Just one torch?

CLEMENT: As far as I remember, one. We had a supply of slightly smaller plastic ones which take the big Eveready battery. They were very unreliable. Often the bulbs wouldn't work or the batteries were flat.

LAWSON: And then you sent them out doing house-to-house enquiries?

CLEMENT: On certain houses. I didn't say, "Knock on every single door." Some houses had their lights on.

LAWSON: Would this be a rather cursory house-to-house enquiry?

CLEMENT: It would have been.

LAWSON: Just explain to me and some of us here as a layman: why was the house-to-house one put after the cursory search of the road? Surely, some might think it would be more important to find out if anybody had said: "Yes, they went that way."

CLEMENT: I don't know why.

LAWSON: Was that a sensible question or suggestion?

CLEMENT: It is a sensible question, yes.

LAWSON: In the weekend immediately following the murder, you remember the apparent thoroughness of the briefings you received?

CLEMENT: Yes.

LAWSON: You said: "I was aware that there were some suspects being mentioned as possibly being involved, but I couldn't remember the names." As you know, sergeant, there has been for some years a great deal of publicity in relation to certain names in this case, so I need not...

CLEMENT: I can't remember what names were mentioned.

LAWSON: Do you recall whether you were told that the Acourts were suspected?

CLEMENT: I can't remember, no.

LAWSON: Have you ever heard of them before?

CLEMENT: I hadn't, no.

LAWSON: Have you heard of the name Norris before, I venture to suggest?

CLEMENT: Yes, yes.

LAWSON: It is somewhat infamous, some might say?

CLEMENT: Yes.

LAWSON: Were you actually told names before you did your house-to-house briefing?

CLEMENT: No.

LAWSON: Would it not have been a good idea if you were going around getting information from people in the neighbourhood if you had known who the supposed suspects were?

CLEMENT: Yes.

LAWSON: But nobody told you that?

CLEMENT: I didn't know the names.

MACPHERSON: So if you had walked into a house and found several Acourts in it, it would not have meant anything to you at all?

CLEMENT: Probably not.

MACPHERSON: It strikes me that in that case your visit to the houses was totally useless?

CLEMENT: The reason – I see what you're saying. I was never aware of the names of the suspects at that early stage of that enquiry.

LAWSON: May we please have back on the screen, still on the house-to-house inquiries, PCA 37, page two, please.

We see, there is in this chronology, the first reference to any of the suspects. At 1.50 pm there is the anonymous male telephoning with information about Neil Acourt and David Norris, do you see that?

CLEMENT: Yes.

LAWSON: During the course of the weekend, as we can see, if more information came in making similar allegations against similar people, as we understand it, none of that was passed to you or those under you carrying out the house-to-house inquiries.

CLEMENT: As far as I can remember, yes, that is the case.

LAWSON: Can we just look back, please, at PCA 37, page two. On Friday the 23rd of April, at 7.45 pm, there is a record of "an anonymous male" – in fact we know him as Grant – "visiting the police station" and alleging specifically, I should say, "that the two Acourt brothers of 102 Bournbrook Road, together with others, were responsible for the murder".

CLEMENT: Yes, I can see that, yes.

LAWSON: That is information that as far as you know was never passed to you?

CLEMENT: Not that I can remember at this time, no.

LAWSON: That is just the sort of information that presumably you would say from your experience that you would want to ensure very promptly got passed to the investigating officer…

CLEMENT: Absolutely, yes.

LAWSON: …for urgent action?

CLEMENT: Yes.

LAWSON: Thank you.

KAMLISH: So that the officer understands:

It is not accepted by the Lawrence family that this officer got to the scene when he claims he did;

It is not accepted he carried out the early searches in the way he claims he did or at all;

It is not accepted that he made the thorough enquiries he claims at the scene;

It is not accepted that he went to the Welcome Inn;

And other parts of his evidence are not accepted from the scene.

Can I first of all ask you about records. Now, you have no records whatsoever compiled by you from the night of the 22nd/23rd of April, do you?

Exit LAWSON.

CLEMENT: That's correct, yes.

KAMLISH: Not a single note?

CLEMENT: Not a single note.

KAMLISH: One record that might assist the inquiry as to whether you are telling the truth about what you did that night and what your vehicles did, would be the so-called tag sheets from the carrier. Yes?

CLEMENT: Yes, I see what you are saying. A tag sheet is just a sheet of paper. There is hundreds of them in a tray so they wouldn't tend to prove anything, really.

KAMLISH: No, but it is a log of what the carrier is doing on a particular occasion?

CLEMENT: Yes, that's right.

KAMLISH: It would record who is on it?

CLEMENT: That's correct, yes.

KAMLISH: You know, do you not, that all the tag sheets for this night for your vehicles have all gone missing?

CLEMENT: I have been informed of this, yes.

KAMLISH: Have you been involved in trying to search for them?

CLEMENT: No.

KAMLISH: When you arrived on the night, who exactly was there?

CLEMENT: I don't know the officers.

KAMLISH: What about a young man in a hysterical state running up and down, shouting, screaming, perhaps arguing a bit in a state of, I suppose, extreme hysteria, standing around and moving around where Stephen was lying?

CLEMENT: No, I never saw him.

KAMLISH: You were not there, were you, at this time?

CLEMENT: Oh yes, I was there.

KAMLISH: I suggest it was impossible to have missed Duwayne Brooks in the state that he has been described if you had been there at the time he was there?

CLEMENT: I was there.

GOMPERTZ: If my learned friend is moving to another topic – I did not want to have to interrupt, and I see that Mr Lawson is not in the chamber at the moment – we are becoming increasingly concerned, sir, about what is happening. This witness was asked to come here without the service of any form of Salmon letter* upon him. All kinds of allegations have been put to him of which he has had no notice whatsoever.

MACPHERSON: If this is going to happen again, I must have notice of it, because fairness works both ways, and if officers are going to be asked questions in the way they are being asked they must be given notice that that is going to happen. Because they may need representation.

---

* In a public inquiry, a *Salmon letter* is the prior written notification given to a witness indicating the specific areas about which they are to be questioned. Named after Lord Salmon's report on tribunals.

What is said now is that officers not only told lies but they have actually invented their presence at the scene.

MANSFIELD: Well, sir, we obviously have all been discussing outside the concerns that we have. I accept in fairness there should be some notice.

MACPHERSON: I am grateful to you.

KAMLISH: You went to Phineas Pett Road, that was one of the roads that was searched?

CLEMENT: Yes, I see that road, yes.

KAMLISH: Can we have Law nine, page 537 up, please. Law 00090537.

Gary Dobson's alibi notice: "Gary Dobson lived with his parents at number 13 Phineas Pett Road." You have no record of having gone to the door of that house nor has anybody else?

CLEMENT: I certainly have no record, no.

KAMLISH: I am just giving this as an example of how your earlier visits to houses could blow somebody's alibi out of the water.

CLEMENT: I agree, of course, yes.

KAMLISH: Your failure to record who you spoke to and the houses you went to would have lost the prosecution the advantage forever, would it not?

CLEMENT: You use the word "failure". I do not think we failed in anything we did on that evening. We were very professional and expedient in our enquiries on that evening.

MACPHERSON: The point is that you did not go to any houses beyond Dickson Road.

KAMLISH: Thank you very much, no further questions.

MACDONALD: One of the things is when a group of attackers disappear off up a side street, they may have a car parked up there which they get into?

CLEMENT: Yes, there is always that possibility, yes.

MACDONALD: So, no doubt, you were on the look-out for cars that might contain youths of that general description?

CLEMENT: Yes.

MACDONALD: You in fact saw such a car, did you not?

CLEMENT: We saw a vehicle, yes. A red vehicle, yes. Drive along Well Hall Road on two occasions on that night.

MACDONALD: A red Vauxhall Astra?

CLEMENT: Yes, that is the case, yes.

MACDONALD: How many people did that vehicle contain?

CLEMENT: From memory, I said it was full of white youths, I believe.

MACDONALD: You would not have logged that car unless there was something suspicious about it, would you?

CLEMENT: That is right, yes.

MACDONALD: You were told the occupants were laughing as they looked on?

CLEMENT: Yes.

MACDONALD: Was that what was suspicious or that they fitted the general description that originally came from Duwayne Brooks of five or six white youths, male?

CLEMENT: That would obviously make you consider this vehicle may have had something to do with it, why they would be laughing?

MACDONALD: A week later you see the same car, do you not?

CLEMENT: Yes.

MACDONALD: And stop it?

CLEMENT: Yes.

MACDONALD: You spoke to the driver and took details, did you not?

CLEMENT: That is the case, yes.

MACDONALD: That was Daniel Copley?

CLEMENT: Yes, aged eighteen.

MACDONALD: Were you aware that Daniel Copley had been convicted in connection with an attack on Nathan and Rolan Adams; he was part of the attacking group which led to the murder of Rolan Adams a little bit earlier?

CLEMENT: What you are telling me now is the first indication of that that I am aware of.

MACDONALD: Ciaran Highland, no one told you that he was a leading light in NTO, the Nazi Turnout, a racist organisation that operates in the Eltham area?

CLEMENT: I was never informed of that either.

MACDONALD: Did anyone tell you from subsequent enquiries that those two who were in the car when you stopped it were in fact in the car on the night in question going past the scene?

CLEMENT: No, I did not speak to anyone about those connections.

MACDONALD: No. You can see the obvious significance of it now, can you not?

CLEMENT: Yes.

MACDONALD: You were never told that those people you had seen, had noted and eventually stopped, were involved in the Rolan Adams inquiry?

CLEMENT: I was never aware of that, no.

MACDONALD: Thank you.

MACPHERSON: Thank you very much.

From the evidence of Helen Avery, 27 March 1998

LAWSON: Your name is Helen Elizabeth Avery?

AVERY: That's right.

LAWSON: You had been out for the evening with your mother and your stepfather, had you not?

AVERY: That's right.

LAWSON: And got back to find, amongst other things, a police car with a flashing light outside your home. When you went to go towards your house, you became aware of Stephen Lawrence, who was lying on the pavement. Correct?

AVERY: Yes.

LAWSON: You knew a bit about first-aid, did you?

AVERY: Yes. I've been a first aider since I was about eleven.

LAWSON: Do you belong to any organisation?

AVERY: Yes. St John's Ambulance.

LAWSON: You actually belong to St John's Ambulance?

AVERY: That's right.

LAWSON: At this stage you were what – what were you, about fifteen?

AVERY: I was just coming up to fourteen.

LAWSON: Fourteen. Anyway, you went inside, yes?

AVERY: Yes.

LAWSON: No doubt obviously you kept an eye on what was going on through the window?

AVERY: That's right, yeah.

LAWSON: Thank you very much.

KAMLISH: I think you actually held a first-aid certificate since you were eleven?

AVERY: That's right, yeah.

KAMLISH: So you get the same training as older people in that first-aid training course?

AVERY: Yes.

KAMLISH: When you have a first-aid training course, stemming the flow of blood is one of the most important features you are taught?

AVERY: Yes.

KAMLISH: Because it can save somebody's life?

AVERY: Yes.

KAMLISH: You never saw anybody either looking for where the blood was coming from or trying to stop the flow?

AVERY: That's right.

KAMLISH: When you first arrived back from where you had been, you actually spoke to a police officer, did you not?

AVERY: That's right.

KAMLISH: Or your stepfather did?

AVERY: Yes, my stepfather did.

KAMLISH: He actually asked one of the officers who was there, was there by Stephen: "Can we be of any assistance?"

AVERY: That's right, he did.

KAMLISH: What did the police officer say?

AVERY: They declined any assistance. They told us that he had been attacked and that the ambulance was on its way.

KAMLISH: But the officers you were talking to were not either then or shortly before or after attending to Stephen himself?

AVERY: No, I didn't see anybody attending to Stephen.

KAMLISH: It is also right, is it not, that you have never been asked to make a statement by the Metropolitan Police?

AVERY: That's right.

KAMLISH: Nor have you ever had a knock on the door and been asked for an account of that night?

AVERY: That's right.

KAMLISH: Nor have you had a message left for you by the police to get in touch with them to tell them what had gone on that night?

AVERY: That's right.

KAMLISH: Thank you very much.

GOMPERTZ: Miss Avery, you went upstairs to join your sister, I think?

AVERY: That's right.

GOMPERTZ: Because she has described a rather different picture to that which you give us – that there was a lady police officer who was either knelt by or crouched over Stephen by the pavement. Do you think that could be right?

AVERY: I could be mistaken, but I don't remember anyone attending to the body. I don't really remember anybody crouching down, but I mean it was a very hectic night. There were a lot of emotions going around.

From the statement of Neville Lawrence, 27 March 1998

MACPHERSON: Mr Mansfield, Mr Lawrence is happy that his statement should be read this morning. Does that suit everybody?

MANSFIELD: Yes.

SOORJOO: (*Statement of Neville Lawrence.*) "I was born on the 13th of March 1942 in Kingston, Jamaica. I came to England in 1960 at the age of eighteen. When I first came here I lived in Kentish Town which at the time was notorious for teddy boys and things like that. I was available to work as an upholsterer because I had done my apprenticeship and was therefore qualified. Unfortunately, I was not able to get a job. I believe this was because of racism. The racism that we experienced then was not as bad as that we now experience. In those days it was mostly verbal, not physical. The violence is much worse nowadays.

"I experienced racism when I first arrived here but I did not recognise it as such at the time. People used to make jokes about us in a way that you did not realise it was actually being racist. They used to call us 'coons' and the like but then you thought it was like a nickname.

"Stephen was born on September 13th 1974 at Greenwich District Hospital. Stephen was very talented at school. His favourite subject was art. One of the things we discovered was that he wanted to be an architect; he was very good at drawing.

"Stephen has never been in trouble. We brought our children up to respect the law. As far as I know, Stephen had never even spoken to a policeman. The children attended Trinity church in Woolwich from an early age. Stephen was christened there.

"In the early 1990s, there were several murders of black people in our area. I had not thought that racism was so bad in the area.

"On the morning of April 22nd 1993 Stephen came into our bedroom overlooking the road and said 'seeya later'. He asked me if I was okay and I said yes. He went down and returned upstairs and said: 'Are you sure you are all right, Dad?' I said, 'yes'. Because I was not working I was not feeling all that good about myself. I watched Stephen go down the road with his rucksack over his back. That is the last time I saw him alive.

"Ten-thirty pm there was a ring at the doorbell. I thought it was Stephen. It was Joey Shepherd. Joey told me that Stephen had been attacked down the road at a bus stop by the Welcome Inn Pub by about six white youths. Doreen called the police who told her that they knew nothing about the incident. We drove to the Brook hospital which was a few minutes away.

"I was just praying that he was not dead. We just sat there. All sorts of things were going through my mind. They came in the door. I do not remember the exact words they used, but I do remember they said that Stephen was dead, we could phone our relatives or something like that. It still did not hit me. When they said Stephen was dead, Duwayne went wild. I just sat there. I was numb.

"Nobody actually told us what happened to Stephen. Nobody. None of the policemen at the hospital spoke to us. I am sure I would have remembered if they did.

"The next day is very cloudy. We still did not know how Stephen had been killed. We were introduced to the two liaison officers, DS Bevan and DC Holden. Holden made a remark about woollen gloves and a hat being found. It was clear she was implying that Stephen was a cat burglar.

"There were incidents where our car tyres were slashed. It made us feel even more threatened.

"We had fears about burying Stephen here because of the situation surrounding his death. In June 1993, we flew out to Jamaica with the body. He is lying beside his grandmother in Clarendon in Jamaica."

From the evidence of Inspector Groves, 1 and 2 April 1998

LAWSON: You're an inspector serving in the Metropolitan Police?

GROVES: Yes, that's right.

LAWSON: Currently serving where?

GROVES: Westminster.

LAWSON: Mr Groves, already on the screen is a copy of the statement made by you in May 1993. The matters you were being asked particularly to address, page 24 of volume 50, it is right there: questions of consideration being given to neglect of duty in respect of failure to ensure a record was kept at the scene and a failure in respect of first-aid treatment?

GROVES: That's right, sir.

LAWSON: Moving back to PCA 38, page 303, may I ask you this – this is obviously dealing with the events of the evening of the 22nd of April 1993 – I understand, is this correct, that you have no surviving notes?

GROVES: No, sir, I have not.

LAWSON: There was reference to you having a clipboard at the scene?

GROVES: I still have the clipboard. I don't have any notes.

LAWSON: What happened to them, do you know?

GROVES: The notes I made that night were fairly comprehensive. They were taken by me at their request to Shooter's Hill Police Station a little while later.

LAWSON: Are you able to give an indication of what time you got to the scene?

GROVES: No, not really, I would think about 10.45.

LAWSON: Would you regard yourself as having been in charge of the scene?

GROVES: Yes.

LAWSON: Had you been given an inkling as to what had happened to Stephen Lawrence, apart from the fact that you had been told he had been assaulted with an iron bar and had serious head injuries?

GROVES: No sir.

LAWSON: Had you asked anybody at the scene if they could assist with what had happened?

GROVES: Yes.

LAWSON: What were you told?

GROVES: I did not have any information.

LAWSON: The very distraught young man who was there was Duwayne Brooks – WPC Bethel managed to calm him down sufficiently to get some account from him about what happened, but that was never passed to you?

GROVES: No, sir, I don't think so. I carried on walking to the pub.

LAWSON: You learned nothing from that?

GROVES: No, nothing at all.

LAWSON: Your account is that a variety of streets in the neighbourhood were directed by you to be searched by police, some with dogs, is that right?

GROVES: The one that happened at midnight, the main search, the very, very, thorough search.

LAWSON: Nothing, in fact, was found, was it?

GROVES: I have a feeling that the only thing one of them found was – I do not think it was anything to do with this. I think it was a salt pot.

LAWSON: Was a report made to you that night about the red Astra. Does that mean anything to you?

GROVES: No, sir. I don't think so. I don't recall.

LAWSON: Thank you.

MANSFIELD: So everybody knows exactly what it is that is being suggested on behalf of Mr and Mrs Lawrence in relation to you, I just want to pick out some of those.

First of all, it is suggested that you failed to take proper control of the scene upon arrival as the first senior officer.

Secondly, you failed to discover relevant information in order to exercise proper control.

Thirdly, that you failed to order and monitor an effective and immediate search for offenders by means of mobile, house-to-house and witness search.

Fourthly, the failure of one to three arose because of your assumptions about the nature of the offence and the victim – race.

The first question I want to ask you, officer, is looking back on it all now, is there anything you think first of all that went wrong as the senior officer between 11 and 1.30 in the morning with the investigation under you?

GROVES: No, sir, I don't think so.

MANSFIELD: Nothing?

GROVES: With the investigation, no.

MANSFIELD: Right. I am going to suggest to you that there was a great deal more that you could have done which might have resulted in something, it might not, do you follow?

GROVES: Yes, sir, certainly.

MANSFIELD: To use your own words to the Kent investigation: "Unless you search an area thoroughly and quickly, then you are losing evidence all of the time"?

GROVES: That's right, sir.

MANSFIELD: And I suggest to you that you were losing evidence every minute that went by that night, were you not?

GROVES: I would absolutely agree with you.

MANSFIELD: Right. So where did it go wrong, officer?

GROVES: Where did what go wrong?

MANSFIELD: Let us start with a fairly basic matter. Which carrier were you on when you went to the scene?

GROVES: I am not sure. The carrier that had Clement on it, 325 I believe.

MANSFIELD: Clement was in charge of 325, was he?

GROVES: Yes.

MANSFIELD: Clement was in charge of 326.

GROVES: Was he?

MANSFIELD: Was he? Well, do not ask me. I am asking you. Before we get going on this, Mr Groves, I am going to suggest this inquiry cannot rely on a single word you are saying. Do you think you are totally unreliable?

GROVES: No, sir.

MANSFIELD: I want to ask you very carefully about those notes. When did you last see them?

GROVES: In 1993.

MANSFIELD: What did you do with them?

GROVES: I took them to Shooters Hill.

MANSFIELD: When?

GROVES: A little while later.

MANSFIELD: When? The same day? The next day? Within a week?

GROVES: I am not sure.

MANSFIELD: I would like you to think.

GROVES: Well, I have thought about it for five years.

MANSFIELD: I am sure you have.

GROVES: You will get the same answer: I am not sure.

MANSFIELD: I suggest there is a very strong possibility that there were never any notes. Do you follow, Mr Groves?

GROVES: Yes, I do.

MANSFIELD: How many sheets were involved, roughly speaking?

GROVES: I don't know, sir. I could not answer that.

MANSFIELD: And the notes have never come to light, have they?

GROVES: No, they haven't.

MANSFIELD: No one has seen these notes with diagrams, dustbins and all the rest of it, no one but you?

GROVES: It would certainly make both our lives very much easier had I got my notes.

MANSFIELD: You talk about photocopying. Now what happened to the photocopies?

GROVES: I keep copies of most documents I think I might need. I certainly think I would have kept copies of this.

MANSFIELD: So where are they?

GROVES: This is five years ago. I have not got my copies any more. I have not got them. It would help not only me but it would help the inquiry if I could find the copies. I have not got them. I cannot say more than that. I have not got them.

MANSFIELD: Have you destroyed them?

GROVES: Very probably, yes.

MANSFIELD: Well, did you, and if so when, and why did you not tell Kent: "I destroyed them"?

GROVES: I cannot recall destroying them.

MANSFIELD: Why would you destroy them?

GROVES: I had no reason to keep them past three years.

MANSFIELD: This case you knew was trundling on in one way or another? You knew that from the publicity?

GROVES: Yes, of course.

MANSFIELD: Is there any possibility, officer, that you just never took any notes that night because you were not that bothered about this incident? Is that a possibility?

GROVES: No. When somebody dies it is something that I remember for the rest of my life. I don't just – whether they are black or white is irrelevant, if that is what you are getting at.

MANSFIELD: When you went to the scene, Mr Groves, you did not treat this as a murder enquiry, did you?

GROVES: I think I certainly did...

MANSFIELD: I want you to think very carefully. The question is, when you first went to the scene, you did not treat this as a murder enquiry, did you?

GROVES: Well, not when Stephen was alive.

MANSFIELD: He was dead, I suggest, when you got there?

GROVES: I don't think he was. When I knew Stephen had died this was something very, very different. It was now a murder inquiry.

MANSFIELD: Let us get utterly clear what you thought about this when you first got to the scene. What did you think about it?

GROVES: I thought that what we were dealing with here was possibly a fight.

MANSFIELD: A fight?

GROVES: Sir, if you keep interrupting me, I shall just slow down. It is important that I am allowed to give my answers here and it is not easy with you interrupting. When I arrived at the scene, I saw an unconscious person and my concern was who had done that to that person and I had to think about what I was going to do about finding the person or persons responsible.

MANSFIELD: I am waiting because I did not…

GROVES: I have finished. Please…

MANSFIELD: Now, may I use these words, which I suggest are your words. When you first got to the scene, it was just an assault and that is all.

GROVES: It was a serious assault. We had to act on the information that we had.

MANSFIELD: I am going to put to you, Mr Groves, that I suggest to you very clearly this is one of your assumptions because it is a black victim, was it not?

GROVES: No, sir. You are accusing me of being a racist now and that is not true. I would like it noted that I do not think that is fair either. You have no evidence that I am racist.

MANSFIELD: If I ask you if you are a racist what will you say?

GROVES: Of course I am not. I could not do my job if I was racist, it would not be possible, it is not compatible.

MANSFIELD: You agree you describe the assault as a fight and you say that was based on information?

GROVES: I think what I said was that is what I thought I was dealing with, an assault, a fight. That is right.

MANSFIELD: I am going to ask you carefully. I am going to suggest this is where the approach or attitude of mind to race is important. You did say before that was the message, that it was a fight. Is that right that you had information or was that an assumption by you?

GROVES: I have now said that five times. I have said five times that the information that I had was this was a fight. Do you want me to say it six times for you, would that make it clearer for you? I am not going to elaborate on this.

MANSFIELD: I suggest to you, Mr Groves, I am going to interrupt, there was no information being fed to the police that this man suffered an injury as the result of a fight?

GROVES: In that case you are wrong.

MANSFIELD: Where did you say it came from?

GROVES: I think the call we got, the original call was possibly from the information room.

MANSFIELD: You see, the information that the inquiry has been told was effectively, an assault with an iron bar, quite different to a fight. In other words, somebody being attacked. That was your information, Mr Groves?

GROVES: Sir, of course, I would agree with you.

MANSFIELD: You translated, I suggest to you, the information of an assault into: black man on pavement involved in fight. Is that a possibility?

GROVES: Of course that is a possibility, absolutely. Absolutely.

MANSFIELD: Yes.

GROVES: It is not an assumption, it is a possibility.

MANSFIELD: If you saw a police officer on the ground with injuries and you had been told about an assault with an iron bar, would you assume a fight?

GROVES: I would have to consider it, of course.

MANSFIELD: Moving forward, you were asked specifically questions about the race issue, were you not, by Kent?

GROVES: Yes.

MANSFIELD: What is the word that you use most regularly to describe non-white people?

GROVES: Black people.

MANSFIELD: Do you?

GROVES: Coloured people.

MANSFIELD: Coloured people is the word you most commonly use, is it not?

GROVES: Okay. I am in a sort of quandary here. He is a white man, that is a coloured woman. (*Indicating.*) What else can I say. I have to make some description. I do not think that is being racist. He is a white man, he is a white man, that is a coloured man. (*Indicating.*)

MANSFIELD: I am going to bring it back to the scene, as it were. Did the thought that night, since you kept your options open, ever come across your mind this was a racist attack?

GROVES: Not initially, no.

MANSFIELD: No.

GROVES: Not until I had enough information to make, using your word, an "assumption".

MANSFIELD: Yes, thank you.

MACDONALD: Were you aware that Duwayne Brooks had told WPC Bethel that as they were coming across the road to attack, they had shouted some racist abuse?

GROVES: No, sir, I was not aware of that.

MACDONALD: "What, what nigger."

GROVES: No, sir.

MACDONALD: You told us that you understood that the injuries that Stephen Lawrence had came from a fight?

GROVES: No, that was the information we had.

MACDONALD: Can I ask you this: is that why you went to the pub?

GROVES: A pub is an absolute mine of information. You can learn more from pubs from people who have had a drink than knocking on doors at 11 o'clock.

MACPHERSON: Thank you very much, Mr Groves.

From the evidence of John Davidson, formerly Detective Sergeant, 24 and 27 April 1998

LAWSON: Your name is John Davidson, is it not?

DAVIDSON: It is, sir.

LAWSON: On the Friday, 23rd April as you can see, there had been various bits of information being received referring in particular to the Acourts. Yes?

DAVIDSON: Yes sir.

LAWSON: One perhaps slightly inaccurately referred to as "an anonymous male" visiting the police station. That is the man who became known as James Grant?

DAVIDSON: I believe so, sir.

LAWSON: The message accuses the Acourts and David Norris of the murder. And you saw Grant on other occasions which appear to be unrecorded?

DAVIDSON: They were recorded. The record of them appears to have gone missing, sir.

LAWSON: As an experienced detective officer, you recognised that there was certainly by the weekend, if not before, more than enough information to justify arrest?

DAVIDSON: I recognised there was more than enough information to arrest them, yes sir, but I wasn't aware that, in fact, there were surveillance units and such set up on the houses. I could only imagine that there were other reasons.

LAWSON: For deferring arrest?

DAVIDSON: For deferring arrest.

LAWSON: Were you involved in the investigation after 1993?

DAVIDSON: I was called back in, as I was in the Regional Crime Squad, and I assisted Mr Mellish in observation and eventual arrest of Norris' father – in order to take him away from the scene and perhaps get witnesses to come forward because there was a big fear in the estate of the Norris name. This man was a very dangerous and frightening individual, sir.

LAWSON: There was a series of photographs showing Dobson and Norris together at a car immediately outside the Acourts' house?

DAVIDSON: I have only been made aware of that within the past three weeks.

LAWSON: Does it not strike you as being absolutely extraordinary, if that is not an inadequate adjective, if the sole purpose of the surveillance operation was to gather evidence of association, no one bothered to tell you about the fact they had evidence of association?

DAVIDSON: I am very surprised. I am shocked that I never was shown the photograph and I don't know the reason why.

LAWSON: Thank you.

MANSFIELD: Did anything strike you about the assault, about the witness statements from people who had been at the scene?

DAVIDSON: In what way, sir?

MANSFIELD: No, no, no, this is my question; did anything strike you stand out, when you read those statements?

DAVIDSON: A boy was murdered, a young lad was murdered by four or five other young lads outside a bus stop, what would strike me about that, sir?

MANSFIELD: I just wondered if it occurred to you that it was a race attack?

DAVIDSON: I do not think in my own mind this was a racist attack. I believe this was thugs attacking anyone, as they had done on previous occasions with other white lads.

MANSFIELD: During the Dobson interview you made it clear that you personally did not think this was a race attack, did you not?

DAVIDSON: By that time I didn't, no sir.

MANSFIELD: That is your view today, is it not?

DAVIDSON: It is, sir.

MANSFIELD: Do you know the Association of Chief Police Officers' definition of a racial incident?

DAVIDSON: No, sir.

MANSFIELD: Has anyone ever told you what it is?

DAVIDSON: I would imagine, from my memory and my experience in a job, a racial incident is one which is caused by or through racism. It can be anything from a shout, to an out-and-out racist attack, but because these lads had attacked whites before, I believed they were thugs. They were described as Krays. They were thugs who were out to kill, not particularly a black person, but anybody, and I believe that to this day that that was thugs – not racism, just pure bloody-minded thuggery.

MANSFIELD: I do not want to debate with you about the nature of racism, but do you recognise that thugs who may kill white people for a variety of reasons, but who kill blacks because they are blacks are committing a racial crime?

DAVIDSON: Yes, sir, I recognise that if they were killed because they were black, that is racist.

MANSFIELD: That is exactly what this case was about but you refused to recognise it, did you not?

DAVIDSON: I still refuse to recognise it, sir. I am very surprised that anybody knows it is about that because it has never been cleared up anyway, sir.

MANSFIELD: I want you to think again about when it was that you were deputed to speak to a particular individual which we all know as James Grant. During the late afternoon or early evening of Friday the 23rd of April this person walked into the front office of Eltham police station. Would you just listen to this sentence: 'DC Budgen interviewed this man initially and later the same day with DS Davidson.' That is Friday the 23rd. Is that possible?

DAVIDSON: No, sir. You have the duty sheets here. You will see that I wasn't on the inquiry until 12 o'clock on Saturday.

EGAN: My learned friend can find them on 00320096 and 00320097.

MACPHERSON: It does bear out in fact what Sergeant Davidson says, does it not?

MANSFIELD: His duty sheet does.

DAVIDSON: I am not going to do something and not put it on the duty sheet. I got paid a lot of money at the time by the police.

MANSFIELD: Please be careful, Mr Davidson.

DAVIDSON: I am very careful, sir. I am not going to do something on a Friday for the police and not show it on the duty sheet on a day I am off playing golf.

MANSFIELD: Really?

DAVIDSON: I would never, ever, go and do something for the police when I was playing golf elsewhere. Good God, what are you suggesting, sir? Are you suggesting that I would falsely say I was somewhere when I was somewhere else?

MACPHERSON: Mr Davidson.

DAVIDSON: I am not here for this, sir. I am not here for this at all.

MACPHERSON: You must calm down because Mr Mansfield is entitled to ask the questions.

DAVIDSON: He is not entitled to suggest I would do that, sir.

MACPHERSON: Take a pause. You have dealt with that point, Mr Mansfield.

MANSFIELD: You do recognise that this person – Grant – is, in fact, providing what has been described as crucial information, is he not?

DAVIDSON: Yes, sir.

MANSFIELD: There is in fact absolutely no record, is there, in relation to any of the meetings – and there are quite a number of them – that you had with this man?

DAVIDSON: That's correct, sir.

MANSFIELD: Why not?

DAVIDSON: The docket went missing, sir.

MANSFIELD: To put it bluntly, you really did not want this informant's material to be effectively followed up. Do you follow the point?

DAVIDSON: I can see what you are suggesting, sir, and I would always give my all in every murder. I don't like your suggestion, sir. I would give everything in every murder to solve it and I don't like the fact you are inferring I would do anything different in this. I am sorry, I don't want to sit and take this, sir. Do I have to sit here? He is accusing me of trying to stop this murder by racism. I have been in loads of incidents…

MACPHERSON: Just stop for the moment.

DAVIDSON: I won't have that, sir, he is accusing me of racism in a public inquiry.

MACPHERSON: Mr Davidson, you must take a pause, if you will. You must know what the suggestion that is made in this case is.

DAVIDSON: I have never been accused directly of racism, sir, and I don't accept it.

Slight pause.

MANSFIELD: Grant then went on to say that he may have found a witness, right?

DAVIDSON: (*Pause.*) Yes, sir.

MANSFIELD: This is somebody who is on a bus, there is a description of the stabbing, where on the body, and who did what?

DAVIDSON: Yes, sir.

MANSFIELD: It names, effectively, Neil Acourt and David Norris stabbing him, does it not?

DAVIDSON: Yes, it names Neil and David, yes sir.

MANSFIELD: So this person, Grant, appears to have found somebody who actually saw the stabbing or part of it?

DAVIDSON: Yes sir.

MANSFIELD: This is extremely important, is it not?

DAVIDSON: Yes sir.

MANSFIELD: Having got some information about somebody on the 27th of April, the person on the bus was not seen until the 19th of May. What is the delay for tracking down and seeing this person?

DAVIDSON: I can't properly tell you, sir. Eventually, his mother, when I saw him, suggested that the lad was open to suggestion. At the end of it, I put him down as undoubtedly a Walter Mitty.

MANSFIELD: Do you have a record of the conversation and meetings with this man?

DAVIDSON: I have nothing, sir.

From the evidence of Detective Constable Linda Holden, 5 May 1998

MACPHERSON: Thank you for coming. I am sorry you have been kept waiting. Miss Weekes will ask you questions on behalf of the inquiry.

HOLDEN: Detective Constable Linda Holden.

MACPHERSON: Thank you. You do not need actually to lean forward over the microphone but bring the microphone close to you and then everybody will hear what you say. But speak up so the stenographer can hear you across the room.

WEEKES: You were one of those officers that received the notice that pointed out: "in your dealings as family liaison officer to Mr and Mrs Lawrence, you failed to provide them with adequate support and information concerning the murder of their son, Stephen on the 22nd of April 1993 and the subsequent police investigation"?

HOLDEN: That's correct.

WEEKES: Did you receive at the time any special training for family liaison?

HOLDEN: No specific training as such but in the manuals there are actually sections of different roles as police officers and there is actually a section for family liaison which tells officers what they would do or what they would expect.

WEEKES: You had not been appointed as family liaison before on any other murder?

HOLDEN: Yes, I had.

WEEKES: Oh?

HOLDEN: In 1991 I was the family liaison officer for a black family whose baby had been thrown into the Thames and a few months later I was the family liaison with an Asian family whose fifteen-year-old had been shot in the head.

WEEKES: So you had some experience with a black family and an Asian family at least two years prior to Stephen Lawrence?

HOLDEN: Yes.

WEEKES: Can I go to the Lawrence family. The relationship with Mr and Mrs Lawrence became very difficult?

HOLDEN: Unfortunately yes, it was very, very difficult, yes. There was so many outside agencies from different sorts of parties. I couldn't – I couldn't really get a close relationship with the family because there seemed to be a lot of barriers put up.

WEEKES: Outside agencies; who were they as far as you knew?

HOLDEN: Well, there was some people from the Anti-Racial Alliance.

WEEKES: Yes.

HOLDEN: There was obviously a solicitor.

WEEKES: Is that Mr Khan?

HOLDEN: That is Mr Khan, yes.

WEEKES: Did Mr Khan put any barriers to your communication with Mr and Mrs Lawrence?

HOLDEN: Yes, he did at times, yes.

WEEKES: Perhaps you will help us. What barriers?

HOLDEN: There were things we needed to know about Stephen's background to try and find out whether he had any enemies, whether he had anyone who did not like him, about his friends, certainly about the girlfriend, and just general different things that could have helped the inquiry.

WEEKES: It is quite important, are you saying that Mr Khan stopped the family giving that information?

HOLDEN: No, not at all.

WEEKES: How was it that it did not get to you because of Mr Khan?

HOLDEN: I felt that sometimes we always had to sort of go through Mr Khan. He would sort of say: "Well, if you speak to me and then I will go back to them," and sometimes you would be waiting for his reply.

WEEKES: But you would get the answer?

HOLDEN: Eventually, we would get the answer, yes.

WEEKES: So the problem was going through Mr Khan?

HOLDEN: Yes.

WEEKES: Not that you were stopped from getting information?

HOLDEN: That's right.

WEEKES: Did you think of speaking direct to Mr Khan or getting the Senior Investigating Officer to have a meeting with yourself and Mr Khan as it was you that appeared to have been having a difficulty with the family liaison. Was that done?

HOLDEN: I don't believe it was, no.

WEEKES: No. Any reason why it was not done?

HOLDEN: I really can't answer that.

WEEKES: Did you provide them with information about the inquiry? For example, when the suspects, five suspects, were to be arrested was it yourself that told the Lawrences before or after the arrest?

HOLDEN: I told them the night before that there was going to be arrests made the following day.

WEEKES: I want to ask you about the use of your mobile phone late at night. One of those occasions was, in fact, by Mr Khan?

HOLDEN: That's correct.

WEEKES: He rang you?

HOLDEN: Yes.

WEEKES: To give you information?

HOLDEN: Yes.

WEEKES: About some suspects?

HOLDEN: Yes.

WEEKES: Did that upset you, irritate you in any way?

HOLDEN: When he phoned I think it was about 12.15 at night. He gave me two names of two suspects. He said to me they were tooled up. By this I took it that he meant they were armed and he said they were going to do a burglary. With that I thought he meant straight away, like that particular night. So I said: "Well, do you mean, now?" He said: "No, that was on the night of the murder." This was now a week later. So I must admit I did say to him, I would put it into the system. There wasn't anything I could do at that time of night.

WEEKES: Did you mind him having your mobile number?

HOLDEN: I didn't actually give him my mobile number.

WEEKES: Did you mind him having your mobile number?

HOLDEN: No.

WEEKES: You expressed a view to the Police Complaints Authority that you did not think there was any need for him to have it. Why did you say that?

HOLDEN: I didn't think there was any need for him to have it but if he had said to me: "May I have your mobile number?", then he could have had it.

WEEKES: It would have been natural, as the solicitor representing the family, that he would have got hold of your mobile?

HOLDEN: Probably if he had asked me but he must have obviously got it from the family which is...

WEEKES: Did you tell him you thought there was no need for him to have it?

HOLDEN: No, I didn't, never.

WEEKES: Alright. If you would wait there.

KAMLISH: You say that you informed the family the night before the arrests that there were going to be arrests the following morning by telephone?

HOLDEN: Yes, I did, yes.

KAMLISH: Where is the truth here? Did you tell them the night before or did you not tell them until the following day after the arrests?

HOLDEN: Sorry, you are right. I didn't tell them about the arrests the night before obviously for operational reasons but I did tell them as soon as we made the arrests the next day. So that is absolutely correct, yes.

KAMLISH: You actually gave your mobile number to Mr Khan on the only occasion you met him at the Lawrence's household on the Sunday, did you not, even though you said in evidence a few moments ago that you did not?

HOLDEN: I know I gave two telephone numbers to the family, but I can't recall giving my mobile number to Mr Khan.

KAMLISH: Can you look at this note, please. It is one of Mr Khan's account slips. Is this your handwriting?

HOLDEN: I can't see it from there. (*Handed.*) That is my handwriting, but that is not my mobile telephone number.

KAMLISH: What you did was on the Sunday you gave him those numbers and you must have written down the wrong number, initially. It is your handwriting?

HOLDEN: That is definitely not my mobile telephone.

KAMLISH: You wrote it?

HOLDEN: That's right, but that it is not my number.

KAMLISH: It is the wrong number?

HOLDEN: That's right.

KAMLISH: You remember there came a time when you were made fully aware of the fact that the Lawrences were dissatisfied with the paucity of information coming from you to them and they became upset about this, did they not?

HOLDEN: That's correct, yes, they did.

KAMLISH: And the plan was to invite them to the incident room?

HOLDEN: That's correct.

KAMLISH: They were told specifically, were they not, that Mr Khan could not come?

HOLDEN: That did not come from me. The decision had been made by the senior officers and it was not for me to go and say to them: "Why are you doing that?"

KAMLISH: It was your job to do precisely that?

HOLDEN: No, it wasn't.

KAMLISH: Perhaps that is a convenient moment.

MACPHERSON: Yes. We will break off now for twenty minutes until 11.25. Do not, of course, talk about the evidence. Thank you very much.

Interval.

HOLDEN: Sir, can I clarify one point about my mobile phone.

KAMLISH: You are going to tell us it was your old number, are you not?

HOLDEN: I am, yes. I had time to reflect that I have actually changed my mobile phone number so that is the correct number.

KAMLISH: That can be the only answer, can it not?

HOLDEN: That's correct, sir.

KAMLISH: What was your view as to the motive for Stephen being killed at the time you were acting as family liaison officer?

HOLDEN: I was obviously aware that it was a racist murder, but what the motive was I couldn't say.

KAMLISH: Is not racism a motive? A motive is racism?

HOLDEN: Yes, that's right.

KAMLISH: Stephen was killed by a bunch of sadistic racists. Do you not accept that?

HOLDEN: I do, but I can't say what was in their minds at the time.

KAMLISH: Do you accept he was killed because he was black?

HOLDEN: I really can't answer that.

KAMLISH: You must have been aware of what the eyewitnesses were saying. Yes?

HOLDEN: Yes, I was but…

KAMLISH: I am sorry for interrupting you, but let me summarise. There were three white people at the bus stop near where Stephen fell, one of whom was a teenager, Jospeh Shepherd?

HOLDEN: Yes.

KAMLISH: Plus Mr Westbrook. And a young French woman?

HOLDEN: I think she was on top of the bus.

KAMLISH: She got on to the bus. According to Mr Westbrook, there were other white people. Do you remember him saying that?

HOLDEN: Yes, yes.

KAMLISH: This group of five or six white youths came straight up to Stephen Lawrence and Duwayne Brooks? Do you remember that evidence?

HOLDEN: Yes I do.

KAMLISH: Then they immediately surrounded them and knifed Stephen, and Duwayne got away. Yes?

HOLDEN: I believe that's correct, yes.

KAMLISH: And in the course of the attack or just before the attack, the words: "What, what nigger" were heard?

HOLDEN: That's correct, yes.

KAMLISH: Yes. So two young black men targeted for no apparent reason but racist language spoken, both of whom were strangers to the five or six white men, were they not? That was clear after a while?

HOLDEN: I believe so, yes.

KAMLISH: Can I ask you again to tell us what you think the motive was for this killing?

HOLDEN: I accept all the circumstances surrounding it and I know what you are saying but I can't say what was in the minds of those thugs that killed him. I don't know what their motive was. I can't answer that.

KAMLISH: Did you treat this as a motiveless killing when you were dealing with the Lawrences? You must have done.

HOLDEN: I think what I believed it to be was a tragic murder of a young man who had everything to live for, whether he was black, white, whatever. That's how I saw it.

KAMLISH: Shortly after the murder there was a press release by the Metropolitan Police Service in which this killing was described as a racist murder?

HOLDEN: Yes.

KAMLISH: You can understand, or can you, the way in which this family would have felt about that. You understand there is more...

HOLDEN: Yes, I do, yes.

KAMLISH: ...there is more suffering, more fear, yes? A community not wanting to express their emotions to white people within days of their son being killed by white people in a racist killing. You can understand all of that, can you?

HOLDEN: Yes, perhaps I can, but I didn't look at the family like that. All I saw them as was a family who had lost their son.

KAMLISH: You do not understand how a black family might feel when their son has been killed in a racist attack then?

HOLDEN: I do. From the age of fifteen months old to the age of seventeen, I was actually brought up in Africa, so I do know and understand black people.

KAMLISH: Does that make you understand white racists in a white, suburban neighbourhood?

HOLDEN: I can't answer what those people were doing on that night. I can't answer that.

KAMLISH: You do not have the point, do you?

HOLDEN: I have got the point, but I can't say what was in their minds.

KAMLISH: Moving to questions that you were asking the Lawrences about Stephen himself. This also caused a problem and was handled extremely insensitively by you, was it not?

HOLDEN: No, it wasn't. We were trying to, the same way we would ask any family, what type of – I mean, I knew the type of person that he was and the type of young lad that he was from what I had heard, but in any enquiry we try to establish what the person is like, whether they have got enemies. It is just basically to get information about him.

KAMLISH: Do you not understand how they would have viewed those sort of questions when the police were accepting from the first day that he was killed in either a motiveless or a racist – or both – attack by people he did not know?

HOLDEN: I'm sure the family would have been very, very upset, but unfortunately with the type of enquiry that we were conducting it was necessary to try and establish any type of information we could find out.

KAMLISH: Why?

HOLDEN: To find out who could have been responsible for his murder, whether there was anyone else that might be involved.

KAMLISH: It went on, did it not? Enquiries and results about Stephen went on. You can see, can you knot how it might hurt the Lawrences that you are asking, not only his school headmaster, but his college principal what sort of person he was, whether he had any enemies? You can understand that, can you not?

HOLDEN: Yes, I can, yes.

From the statement of Duwayne Brooks, 1 May 1998

MACPHERSON: Mr Menon, Mr Duwayne Brooks sits beside you?

MENON: On my left, sir.

MACPHERSON: We are very glad that he has come and we are grateful for his assistance. Thank you very much, Mr Brooks. Mr Menon, I understand, will read the statements of Mr Brooks. Thank you very much.

MENON: (*Reads.*) "Stephen Lawrence was one of my best friends. We met on our first day of secondary school – the Blackheath Bluecoats Church of England School. Both Stephen and I were eighteen when Steve was murdered. We saw each other regularly…"

MACPHERSON: I am so sorry to interrupt. Can you go a little slower because it has to be taken down.

MENON: "In the evening we were hurrying to get home as soon as possible. We were just looking for a bus on Well Hall Road. We were attacked by a group of white boys, one of whom shouted 'What, what nigger?' I can't bear to go into the details…

"As were we running from the attack, Steve fell to the floor. I stopped on the pavement. I went back and I bent down and looked at him. He was lying by a tree. He was still breathing. He could not speak. I saw his blood running away.

"I ran across to the phone box and dialled 999. I asked for an ambulance. I left the phone hanging to run round the corner to see if the boys were coming back up the road.

"I saw a white couple. I have since been told they are called Taaffe. They just ignored me. They looked at me and sort of shimmied away. I see he thought we might be going to rob them. A car stopped by Steve. I now know the driver was an off-duty policeman, Mr Geddis, who was with his wife.

"I was pacing up and down, up and down. I was desperate for the ambulance. It was taking too long. I was frightened by the amount of blood Steve was losing. I saw his life fading away. I didn't know what to do to help him. I was frightened I would do something wrong.

"WPC Bethel said, 'How did it start? Did they chase you for nothing?' I said one of them shouted, 'What, what nigger?'

"She asked me if I had any weapons on me. She was treating me like she was suspicious of me, not like she wanted to help. If she had asked me of more details of the boys' descriptions or what they were wearing I would have told her. Those would have been sensible questions.

"None of the uniformed officers were doing anything for Steve. They should have known what to do. They should have done something for Steve. They just stood there doing nothing.

"The ambulance arrived. They carried Steve to the ambulance on a stretcher. His unopened ginger beer can fell from him on to the floor. I picked it up. I took it home and kept it in my room, until one day it exploded. I am told I called the police 'pigs' and used the word 'c…t'. I did not. I don't use those words.

"I was driven to Plumstead Police Station. I now know that in their statements the police said I broke a window in the front office. I didn't. I wasn't even in the front office. It just shows they were treating me like a criminal and not like a victim. They kept saying, 'Are you sure they said, "What, what nigger?"' I said, 'I am telling the truth.' A senior officer said, 'You mean you have done nothing wrong to provoke them in any way?' I said, 'No, we were just waiting for a bus.'

"On the 8th of May, I went to a large anti-racist demonstration outside the British National Party headquarters in Welling. I went to protest against Steve's murder and the way the police were handling it. In October 1993, I was arrested and charged with offences arising out of the demonstration. They waited until the Crown Prosecution Service had decided to drop the prosecution against the killers. It was devastating. It felt like the police and prosecutors decided to get at me to ruin my reputation – and the chance of any future prosecution for the murders. But the judge at Croydon Crown Court wasn't having any of it. In December 1994, he stopped the prosecution saying it was an abuse of the process of the court.

"I think of Steve every day. I'm sad, confused and pissed about this system where racists attack and go free but innocent victims like Steve and I are treated as criminals and at the outset ignored me when I pointed out where the killers had run and refused to believe me that it was a racist attack.

"I never knew Steve to fight no-one. Steve wasn't used to the outside world. He wasn't street-aware of the dangers of being in a racist area at night-time. I shouted to run. He had ample time to run as the boys were on the other side of the road. Steve didn't understand that the group of white boys was dangerous.

"I was taken to the identification parade. I saw a skinhead there, Stacey Benefield. He said the boys who stabbed him were known to stab people and not to get done for it. He said they knew people in the police. I now know that the person I picked out was Neil Acourt.

"On the third identification parade, I now know I identified Luke Knight. Sergeant Crowley said something to the effect that I was guessing. I got angry. I recognised the attackers from the attack and not from any outside information. Nobody described the Acourt brothers to me. I did not know how important Sergeant Crowley's lies were until I heard it on the news that the two men who had been arrested had been released and it was to do with my evidence not being good enough.

"I never told the officer that friends told me descriptions of the people to identify before any parade. If the officer has said I could not identify Stephen's attackers by their faces, he has misunderstood what I said. During the course of general conversation, I said to the officer that I was anti-police and that I wanted to seek revenge for Stephen's death myself and also that I had only called for an ambulance on the night of the murder and not the police.

"I wanted to put down that Sergeant Crowley was a liar, but the officer would not write that down. I recognised the attackers from the attack, not from any outside information."

From the evidence of Detective Inspector Bullock, 18 and 19 May 1998

LAWSON: Benjamin Bullock, I believe you still hold the rank of detective inspector, do you not, in the Metropolitan Police Force?

BULLOCK: Yes, sir.

LAWSON: You were appointed the Deputy Senior Investigation Officer fairly early on the 23rd of April 1993?

BULLOCK: That's correct.

MENON: Mr Bullock, you do appreciate that a large number of what were material decisions in this case do not appear to have been recorded in the policy file?

BULLOCK: That is correct, sir.

LAWSON: As the weekend wore on, there became certain named prime suspects, did there not?

BULLOCK: Yes, sir.

LAWSON: The Acourt brothers, Dobson and Norris, in particular?

BULLOCK: Yes, sir.

LAWSON: During the course of Saturday the 24th of April the investigating team received sufficient information to justify making arrests, had you not?

BULLOCK: We had sufficient information to give reasonable ground, yes sir.

LAWSON: You could have arrested, made some arrests on the Saturday?

BULLOCK: Yes, sir.

LAWSON: The decision was not to arrest. Why was that?

BULLOCK: We had no evidence up to then.

LAWSON: But you could, in your opinion, lawfully have arrested, is that right?

BULLOCK: Yes sir.

LAWSON: You had information on the night of Friday the 23rd that the Acourt brothers did live at 102 Bournbrook Road. Mr Bullock, the justification you gave for not affecting arrests, that you had insufficient knowledge of the Acourts' address, do you think on reflection that really holds water?

BULLOCK: No, we had information of their address, but we couldn't verify that by other means.

LAWSON: Over these first few days what inquiry did you make about the Acourts, Norris, Dobson, racist attacks in the area. You were receiving information from a variety of sources?

BULLOCK: Yes, sir.

LAWSON: Saying they were a violent, nasty bunch?

BULLOCK: Yes.

LAWSON: Did you see whether there was any similar information available from police officers?

BULLOCK: Yes, I am sure we did, sir.

LAWSON: Then information was received which contains at least a positive prospect of an eyewitness being found. There still seems to be an unreasonable delay in doing anything about it, yes?

BULLOCK: Yes, sir.

LAWSON: Why is that?

BULLOCK: I have no answer for that.

LAWSON: No answer?

BULLOCK: No answer.

LAWSON: It does seem a chapter of disasters?

BULLOCK: That's correct.

LAWSON: Let us go to Friday the 30th, to PCA00320009, please.

There is a note suggesting that one of the sources had actually seen Norris and the Acourts in the vicinity on the night of the murder? Again important information?

BULLOCK: Yes sir.

LAWSON: Again requiring action?

BULLOCK: Yes sir. Unfortunately none of these people put this in writing after a number of attempts.

LAWSON: The 6th of May, this is the eve of the arrests, is it not?

BULLOCK: Yes, sir.

LAWSON: What prompted the decision to arrest on the 7th?

BULLOCK: A knife being found, and also a witness who comes out with a remark of "J" or "Jamie".

LAWSON: The arrests took place in the form of dawn raids?

BULLOCK: That's correct.

LAWSON: I want to ask you about knives, please. The Acourts and/or Norris, yes, were fascinated by knives and usually hide them under the floorboards?

BULLOCK: Yes, sir.

LAWSON: What instructions were given for looking under floorboards?

BULLOCK: I don't think there were instructions given to look under the floorboards but the team that was at that address did pull away carpet to look if floorboards were loose, etcetera, but I don't think people went in and just jimmied up floorboards.

LAWSON: You allocated your most experienced sergeant, Davidson, to Dobson, did you not? Did you brief him about the surveillance operation that had been carried out?

BULLOCK: I am not certain if he knew who was involved in the pictures from the surveillance.

LAWSON: He has told us that no one told him anything about them?

BULLOCK: I didn't know Norris was in the photograph.

LAWSON: Do you not think you could or should have found out who Norris was by the time he was arrested and being interviewed?

BULLOCK: I obviously would have liked to, sir. That is why we carried on observations at 102.

LAWSON: Let me ask you, please, about the Grant information coming in. You showed little or no interest in this information when it was being reported to the police station on the Friday night?

BULLOCK: There was interest in the message but at the time I was up to my eyeballs in other things.

LAWSON: But the information he was giving was potentially of great significance, was it not?

BULLOCK: Yes sir.

LAWSON: Not only identifying or purporting to identify the Acourts as being responsible for the murder of Stephen Lawrence, but implicating them in other violent assaults.

BULLOCK: Yes sir.

LAWSON: And it merited your immediate attention, did it not, as the Senior Investigating Officer on duty?

BULLOCK: If I have one regret it is that I didn't see Grant.

LAWSON: Mr Bullock, the arrests on the 7th of May, were there extraneous considerations, that is not connected to the evidence or information, pressures from outside, that contributed?

BULLOCK: No, sir.

LAWSON: You were presumably aware of Mr Mandela's much publicised visit on the 6th?

BULLOCK: Yes sir.

LAWSON: And you were aware of the threatened demonstrations which took place on the 8th of May?

BULLOCK: I believe I was, yes.

LAWSON: And you were obviously aware that there had been well-publicised criticism of the police, including complaints from the family, for inactivity?

BULLOCK: Yes, sir.

LAWSON: Did any of those factors have any bearing at all on the decision that was made?

BULLOCK: No, not at all.

LAWSON: With hindsight, is it the case, do you think, that the arrest should have been made more promptly?

BULLOCK: If I had to do it again sir, then yes, I would agree they should have been made more promptly.

LAWSON: You are speaking very quietly. Can the witness be heard by everyone? It was a racist attack?

BULLOCK: Yes, yes, without a doubt.

LAWSON: Let me ask you this: you referred to the victims of the assault, Stephen Lawrence and Duwayne Brooks, as the two young coloured lads?

BULLOCK: Yes.

LAWSON: Do you understand now that using the expression "coloured" is regarded as offensive?

BULLOCK: I didn't know that before, sir.

MANSFIELD: Officer, as you are aware, I represent Mr and Mrs Lawrence. Looking back over the first weekend and throughout the two vital weeks thereafter and for a longer period, what things do you think you would change?

BULLOCK: I would say an earlier arrest, I would have deployed somebody with that surveillance team, I would have tried to meet the family, obviously tried to contain the media a bit more.

MANSFIELD: The media?

BULLOCK: Try and use Mr Mandela in a positive way with the police. He could perhaps have appealed for witnesses, I don't know.

MANSFIELD: I want to turn to surveillance. The whole operation starting on the Monday really was a complete waste of time, money and resources and, effectively helped to delay arrest. Do you follow, that is the suggestion?

BULLOCK: I did say to you, sir, one of my regrets is that I did not put an officer with the surveillance team.

MANSFIELD: The whole operation would not have been improved by one officer being added to it. I am going to suggest root and branch, the whole operation was a nonsense start to finish, the way you did it.

BULLOCK: It wasn't, sir.

MANSFIELD: There is no tasking document from you that still exists?

BULLOCK: As you say, it doesn't exist, sir.

MANSFIELD: You see, Mr Davidson and others have said, effectively, if only they had known about photographs in the interview with Dobson, they would have used them. Do you follow? Can you explain how Mr Davidson was completely in the dark?

BULLOCK: I can't, no.

MANSFIELD: Unless, of course, the surveillance was really a sham, was it? Was it a sham? Did you really not want to use it?

BULLOCK: That's not true.

MANSFIELD: Where is the record of evaluation by you, namely, this shows Neil Acourt doing so and so. This shows a bin bag leaving the premises. Any record of that?

BULLOCK: I don't think so.

MANSFIELD: Why not?

BULLOCK: I don't think I made a record.

MANSFIELD: Why not, officer?

BULLOCK: I have no answer for that, sir.

MANSFIELD: You knew the name Norris was a criminal name but it has not rung any bells that this man could in any way be related to the famous or notorious, rather, name. That is your position?

BULLOCK: Yes.

MANSFIELD: You did not have an idea of what Norris looked like before he was arrested?

BULLOCK: That's correct.

MANSFIELD: Photographs, bin bags, removing clothing – by the Monday morning, the 26th, you had plenty of material to affect an arrest, did you not?

BULLOCK: Yes.

GOMPERTZ: Mr Bullock, on behalf of the Commissioner, if I may. What is being suggested in this inquiry is that there was a corrupt conspiracy between officers charged with the investigation of the murder of Stephen Lawrence to pursue that inquiry as their duty required they should, to drag their feet, putting it at its lowest, and to try and ensure that David Norris at least, and perhaps other defendants, escaped prosecution. Do you understand that?

BULLOCK: That is totally wrong, sir, totally wrong and offensive.

From the evidence of Mr Ilsley, formerly Detective Chief Cuperintendent, 2–4 June 1998

LAWSON: Mr Ilsley, you remained Detective Chief Superintendent in charge of the on-going Stephen Lawrence investigation?

ILSLEY: That is correct, sir, yes.

LAWSON: Mr Ilsley, you in fact have expressed yourself to be angered and outraged by allegations made, that the investigation was affected by racism and/or collusion with a known criminal?

ILSLEY: That's correct, yes.

LAWSON: Do you acknowledge that there were serious deficiencies in the first murder investigation?

ILSLEY: I acknowledge there were deficiencies in the first murder investigation, yes, sir.

LAWSON: And serious or significant deficiencies?

ILSLEY: Significant I think is the right word.

LAWSON: You were aware, indeed you were part of the Barker review?

ILSLEY: Yes, sir.

LAWSON: You remember, presumably, his reporting that the investigation, the first investigation, had been progressed satisfactorily and all lines of enquiry correctly pursued?

ILSLEY: Yes, sir.

LAWSON: That is not tenable, is it?

ILSLEY: That's correct, sir.

LAWSON: You met with the Lawrences on the 6th of May, did you not?

ILSLEY: Yes, I did sir, yes.

LAWSON: There was handed to you this note which contained a list of suspects, is that right?

ILSLEY: That's correct, sir, yes.

LAWSON: And you know that Mrs Lawrence, in particular, was distressed because you appeared, in effect, to scrumple it up as if you were going to throw it away?

ILSLEY: That's correct, sir, yes.

LAWSON: She said, having handed the note to you, she saw you fold the paper up so small she found shocking. In fact, the original note is available. Can you take it please. (*Handed.*) It does bear the signs of having been folded and folded and folded again into a tiny piece of paper?

ILSLEY: Yes, sir, it does.

LAWSON: Do you think you must have done that, in fact?

ILSLEY: I certainly did, sir, yes.

LAWSON: Was that just you being blunt, tactlessness?

ILSLEY: Not tactlessness, no, sir.

LAWSON: It appeared you were not treating it seriously from what she could see?

ILSLEY: No, I dispute this. I think Mrs Lawrence has said that I screwed it up. I didn't screw it up. I folded it. Why I folded it like that, I don't know, but it went straight into the system.

LAWSON: What Mrs Lawrence said is: "He rolled the piece of paper up in a ball in his hand. I was shocked by what I saw."

ILSLEY: I didn't do that, sir.

LAWSON: But you did fold it up?

ILSLEY: I did fold it, absolutely, sir.

LAWSON: Could you pass it to the chairman, please. (*Handed.*) Is what you are telling us that you were not intending to be dismissive of this information?

ILSLEY: Certainly not, sir, no. How could I be dismissive?

LAWSON: The point, Mr Ilsley, is that you gave the appearance of at least of not treating it seriously?

ILSLEY: Why? By folding it up like that, sir?

LAWSON: Yes.

ILSLEY: I am sorry if I did, but it wasn't intentional in any way whatsoever. What can you say? How you fold something up is how you fold it up. According to Mrs Lawrence, I screwed it up into a ball, which I didn't do.

LAWSON: In due course, on the 6th of May, a decision was made to arrest?

ILSLEY: Yes.

LAWSON: And the basis for that decision was recorded.

Can we look, please, at PCA00450205: "One. All are known associates"?

ILSLEY: Yes

LAWSON: "Two. Artist's impression, similar to Acourts"?

ILSLEY: Yes.

LAWSON: "Three. Information from numerous sources", yes?

ILSLEY: That's correct, sir, yes.

LAWSON: "Four. Norris and possibly others thought to possess a knife". "Five. Strong possibility they were in the area around the time of the murder"?

ILSLEY: Yes, sir.

LAWSON: In terms of information that had been available most, if not all, of those grounds existed the previous two weeks, did they not?

ILSLEY: Yes, sir.

LAWSON: That is all I wish to ask this witness. Just before Mr Mansfield, if you will forgive me, one of your advisors has helpfully suggested it might be sensible *vis-à-vis* the note if I just ask Mr Ilsley to refold it in apparently the way in which it was folded up. (*Short pause.*) Hold it up so everyone can see it. Thank you very much.

MACPHERSON: I have a bit of useless information for you, that you cannot do it more than 8 times, however large the sheet of paper.

MANSFIELD: If there had not been first a complaint by Mr and Mrs Lawrence, you would still be saying there was nothing wrong with the first investigation, would you not?

ILSLEY: I would, sir, yes.

MANSFIELD: That is, to say the least of it, a very unhappy and unsatisfactory situation?

ILSLEY: It is, sir, yes.

MANSFIELD: You agree with all of that?

ILSLEY: I do, sir, yes.

MANSFIELD: I think you agree that reveals a shocking state of affairs, does it not?

ILSLEY: Yes, sir.

MANSFIELD: In the Metropolitan Police?

ILSLEY: At that particular time, sir, yes.

MANSFIELD: It was perfectly proper and obvious that you could have arrested the first weekend?

ILSLEY: Absolutely.

MANSFIELD: You had the legal powers to do it?

ILSLEY: Yes, sir.

MANSFIELD: Nobody would be criticising you for an arrest even if you did not have all the evidence, would they?

ILSLEY: No, sir.

MANSFIELD: The real day you could have gone in, it does not require hindsight, was Monday the 26th?

ILSLEY: I accept that, sir.

MANSFIELD: That happens to be the day on which the first plastic bag disappears before the cameraman is able to set up his camera?

ILSLEY: Yes, sir.

MANSFIELD: That was the day, had you gone in, you would have been in a much stronger position to recover the clothing which might contain fibres – every chance of gathering the smallest amount of evidence has to be taken, does it not?

ILSLEY: I accept what you are saying, yes, sir.

MANSFIELD: I want to deal with Mr Grant, the man we know as Grant. Grant provided the first information to police as to who was responsible for the murder of Stephen Lawrence.

ILSLEY: Yes, sir.

MANSFIELD: Do you know what Grant is saying happened with the Met? He is complaining that from the beginning he told the Met, your officers, who the source was for the information and the identity of somebody who was a witness. Did you know that?

ILSLEY: No, sir.

MANSFIELD: "Hasn't given us anything, won't pay him £50, uncooperative." That was your view of Grant?

ILSLEY: That was my view at that particular time.

MANSFIELD: Your view is that you did not want Grant at the forefront of this investigation because he was too hot to handle?

ILSLEY: What does that mean, sir?

MANSFIELD: He knew too much and you did not want to arrest at the first weekend, so Grant had to be kept out?

ILSLEY: How ludicrous. That is absolutely disgusting that you say something like that, sir.

MANSFIELD: I am going to suggest to you there is only one inference, because of your lack of action and information, do you follow, Mr Ilsley?

ILSLEY: What are you saying, sir? Are you saying that I am corrupt?

MANSFIELD: I am suggesting very clearly that you did not in fact use the very person who was prepared to give you precise information. The very thing you claimed you put off the arrests for was neglected and kept out of the way essentially?

ILSLEY: Because I am corrupt, that is what you are saying.

MANSFIELD: Do you think you are corrupt; is that what you are saying?

ILSLEY: That is what you are saying, sir.

MANSFIELD: You see, Mr Davidson – you are perhaps not aware of this – agrees that a name was given by Grant and an address.

ILSLEY: Well, I didn't know that, sir.

MANSFIELD: That message is a description of a stabbing whereby Norris commits a stab wound and so does Neil Acourt. Do you follow?

ILSLEY: Okay sir, I accept that.

MANSFIELD: It is important. It is somebody claiming to have seen two assailants attack Stephen Lawrence?

ILSLEY: Yes.

MANSFIELD: You are saying, are you, that you never knew that Grant had actually provided you with the name of an eyewitness?

ILSLEY: No, sir, only afterwards did I know, but not during the investigation, no.

MANSFIELD: You never knew it came from Grant?

ILSLEY: I didn't, sir, no.

MANSFIELD: Until now, today?

ILSLEY: Until today, yes.

MANSFIELD: Were you aware a Metropolitan Police Officer was consorting with Clifford Norris?

ILSLEY: No, sir.

MANSFIELD: Are you sure?

ILSLEY: Positive. I can't remember that. I might have known at any time. I can't remember it now.

MANSFIELD: We are calling "XX". It would be completely out of order for that officer to have meetings with Clifford Norris on the pretext of nurturing him as an informant; that would be completely out of order?

ILSLEY: It would, sir. Totally. Especially as a professional criminal, yes.

MANSFIELD: You became aware that David Norris was the son of Clifford Norris?

ILSLEY: Yes.

MANSFIELD: Did you then decide: "Well, one of the things we better do perhaps in this case since Clifford Norris is wanted, is to make sure we arrest him and get him off the scene." Did that occur to you?

ILSLEY: No sir.

MANSFIELD: Why not?

ILSLEY: Well, he is a wanted man.

MANSFIELD: Yes, why not get him arrested fast?

ILSLEY: If he could have been arrested he would have been arrested fast. I assume once someone is wanted, they are wanted.

MANSFIELD: You see, perhaps you cannot answer the question of how it is that he stays at large and then when a senior officer takes over from you, Mr Mellish, decides that the time has come to remove the Norris threat, he is then arrested. Can you help us as to how it is that Clifford Norris stays at large?

ILSLEY: I can't, sir. We were under tremendous pressure as far as resources were concerned.

MANSFIELD: You had a wonderful opportunity to get David Norris off the streets, did you not, in this case?

ILSLEY: Yes.

MANSFIELD: You knew by the Monday that Clifford Norris was related?

ILSLEY: I probably did, yes.

MANSFIELD: We go to the 6th of May, a final decision about an arrest. Was it being done in a rush for a particular reason, Mr Ilsley?

ILSLEY: Not as far as I know sir, no.

MANSFIELD: I would like you to think carefully. The 6th was a particularly important day, was it not?

ILSLEY: The Nelson Mandela…

MANSFIELD: That is right. It had a massive effect – your words – on the publicity in relation to this case?

ILSLEY: It did sir, yes.

MANSFIELD: It was not a good effect from your point of you, was it?

ILSLEY: You are probably right, sir, yes. We had not arrested anyone, that's right.

MANSFIELD: It is not good news to have perhaps one of the world's foremost statesman in London and picking up the fact that a squad under your command have not managed to pick somebody up. That is not good news from a public relations point of view, is it?

ILSLEY: I can see what your saying, yes, sir.

MANSFIELD: In relation to race. In this case, if anybody in your squad were to say that it wasn't racially motivated, that would beggar belief, would it not?

ILSLEY: As far as I was concerned it was a racially motivated crime and it was obvious from day one. As far as the other people are concerned, they have got to answer for themselves.

MANSFIELD: There was a great attempt by Davidson, Holden and others in this inquiry to try and make a distinction between a racist murder and racially motivated murders and so on, do you follow?

ILSLEY: I do sir.

MANSFIELD: Do you find that reprehensible?

ILSLEY: I find it incredible, yes.

MANSFIELD: You find it incredible. Thank you.

MENON: Mr Ilsley, I ask questions on behalf of Duwayne Brooks.

ILSLEY: Yes, sir.

MENON: When XX was interviewed he said the various meetings with Clifford Norris in public houses was by pure chance and that, although unauthorised by any senior officer, he was meeting Mr Norris for the purpose of cultivating him as an informant. That is what he told the internal inquiry. That inquiry concluded that there was more to the relationship between XX and Clifford Norris than XX was prepared to admit?

ILSLEY: Yes, sir.

MENON: Yet for reasons best known to that internal inquiry, they chose not to discipline him, but simply give "words of advice"?

ILSLEY: Yes.

MENON: Bringing it back closer to home, XX, we have discovered recently, guarded Duwayne Brooks on at least one night during the period of the private prosecution. Can you think of any less appropriate officer in the Metropolitan Police to have been chosen to protect

Duwayne Brooks whilst he is giving evidence at the Old Bailey as part of the private prosecution?

ILSLEY: If the facts are what you say and I accept they are true, yes, I do, sir, I find it incredible.

From the statement of Doreen Lawrence, 11 June 1998

LAWSON: Sir, the proposal now is to invite the completion of the reading of Mrs Lawrence's statement, and then for the questioning of Mrs Lawrence.

MACPHERSON: Mrs Lawrence, thank you very much for being here. There is a glass of water there should you wish it. If you want to pause at any time let me know, will you not? Do not hesitate to tell me.

BOYE-ANAWOMA: I am going to carry on reading Mrs Lawrence's statement.

(*Reads.*) "The police were not interested in keeping us informed about the investigation. We were simply regarded as irritants.

"It was also claimed that the police found dealing with our solicitor a hindrance. Basically, we were seen as gullible simpletons. This is best shown by Ilsley's comment that I had obviously been primed to ask questions. Presumably, there is no possibility of me being an intelligent, black woman with thoughts of her own who is able to ask questions for herself. We were patronised and we were fobbed off. As the meetings went on, I got more and more angry. I thought that the purpose of the meetings was to give us progress reports, but what actually happened was that they would effectively say: stop questioning us. We are doing everything. That simply was not true, and it led me to believe then and now that they were protecting the suspects.

" In September 1993 we hoped to get some feedback from the Barker review. We met with him too. He said that he couldn't give us a copy of the report, but he promised that we would meet again so that he could tell us what he had found out. That was the first and last time we ever saw him. The second investigation started with meeting Commissioner Condon in April 1994. We discussed the Barker review, and that was the first time we met Ian Johnston. We were still kept in the dark about some things in the second investigation. We weren't told exactly what was happening, but we heard rumours that things had gone wrong with the first investigation, and I think there was some cover-up about what was going on. It was then decided that the Crown Prosecution Service wouldn't take matters further. I felt we had no choice but to take a private prosecution, and I don't believe they would have been acquitted if we could have presented everything to the jury. On the first day at the Old Bailey I was extremely optimistic, but from the minute the judge opened his mouth, my hopes were dashed. It was clear from the outset he had come with the intention of not letting the matter proceed further. The judge instructed them to return a verdict of not guilty. When he told them that there was no alternative they actually went outside to consider it and then came back in. They didn't want to do it.

"I believe that the Kent Police Complaints Authority Report has not got to the bottom of what went on, it scratched the surface. At the beginning the Kent Police Complaints Authority Report was saying that the police officers were not racist in their attitude. If it wasn't racism what was it? Incompetence? Corruption? That only goes some way to explain. We are told these officers have years of experience investigating murders. What went wrong? Something did. Their attitude tells me that it was racism.

"It has been suggested that we were telephoned on the morning of the 7th of May 1993 to be told of imminent arrests. We had a meeting with Ilsley on the evening of the 6th of May and nothing was told to us or mentioned either. We complained then to senior officers that we had not been notified of an arrest in advance and, on the second arrest date, we were telephoned. We assumed first. Half an hour later we saw it on the television.

"I would like Stephen to be remembered as a young man who had a future. He was well loved and had he been given the chance to survive maybe he would have been the one to bridge the gap between black and white; he just saw people as people."

MACPHERSON: Mrs Lawrence, there is just one matter I would like you to clarify. There has been a lot of debate over the incident with the information you gave to Mr Ilsley in note form and what exactly happened. I wonder if you could just decide for everybody what happened to that piece of paper?

MRS LAWRENCE: On the evening when we went to the police station, as I walked in, at the time I didn't know his name, I handed the piece of paper with the names on to this officer. He took the paper from me, he folded it in small pieces in his hand, and then he had it in his hands like this, crunched up in his hand like a ball, and he held it like that, and as I was walking out through the door, I said to him: "You are going to put that in the bin now, aren't you?" And he was shocked because he didn't realise I was watching him, and he quickly said: "No, we treat all information that comes to the police."

GOMPERTZ: Mrs Lawrence, I want to ask you some questions on behalf of the Commissioner. In doing so can I make it absolutely clear that my purpose is not to criticise you and your husband. Secondly can I make it clear that I am mindful of the Chairman's ruling that was made a long time ago that counsel who wish to ask you and your husband questions should confine themselves to matters of fact and not opinion.

Can I ask you please to look at your note. Those are the names, are they not, that you wrote on the piece of paper and took with you when you went to see Mr Ilsley?

MRS LAWRENCE: Yes.

GOMPERTZ: You see, the reason I ask you is that if all the names were written on this piece of paper, they did not include the names Norris or Knight, did they?

MRS LAWRENCE: No, people were confused about the names when they came to us.

GOMPERTZ: Can I ask you about something quite different now: your journey home from the hospital on the night in question. You went, did you not, to the Welcome Inn?

MRS LAWRENCE: No.

GOMPERTZ: Where did you go then?

MRS LAWRENCE: Can I ask a question here? Am I on trial here or something here? I mean, from the time of my son's murder I have been treated not as a victim. Now I can only tell you or put into my statements what I know of went on that night. And for me to be questioned in this way, I do not appreciate it.

MACPHERSON: Mr Gompertz, I think your discretion should be exercised in favour of not asking further questions.

GOMPERTZ: Sir I will, of course, accept your guidance.

MACPHERSON: Thank you.

EGAN: Can I just ask one matter of Mrs Lawrence, please.
Do you remember you had a conversation with Holden,
one of the police officers tasked with family liaison and,
as a result, she delivered a birthday card to your
daughter who was on an outward bound course. Do you
remember that?

MRS LAWRENCE: Yes.

EGAN: Why do you think she did that?

MRS LAWRENCE: She wanted to be helpful.

MR MCDONALD: We have no questions.

MACPHERSON: Thank you very much, Mrs Lawrence.

From the evidence of William Mellish, formerly Detective Superintendent, 11, 15 and 16 June 1998

LAWSON: We are now leaving what might be called the
first investigation and going into the second, which was
conducted by Mr Mellish.

MACPHERSON: Mr Lawson, on behalf of the inquiry, will
question you first.

MELLISH: Yes, sir.

LAWSON: Mr Mellish, we are grateful to you for
volunteering your assistance to the inquiry. It is right, is
it not, to say you were not involved in the investigation
that was carried out by the Kent police.

MELLISH: That is correct.

LAWSON: No complaint or allegation having been made
against you or relating to the second investigation?

MELLISH: No, sir.

LAWSON: Mr Mellish, it was in the middle of 1994, was it not, that you assumed the mantle of Senior Investigating Officer?

MELLISH: Yes, sir.

LAWSON: Can I ask you in the most general terms, your own experience of racism within the Metropolitan Police Force?

MELLISH: I would say there is some racism in some officers, in a minority of officers.

LAWSON: Over your last ten years, did it get better, get worse, or stay much the same, would you say?

MELLISH: I would say much the same.

LAWSON: Your investigation – you decided to take an entirely fresh approach? No one had been prosecuted to conviction.

MELLISH: Yes.

LAWSON: You were aware this was racially motivated?

MELLISH: Yes, sir.

LAWSON: By virtue of Duwayne Brooks' evidence of the shout of, "What, what nigger", before the gang attacked?

MELLISH: Yes, sir.

LAWSON: Your belief that this was a racially motivated murder was hardened up as a result of the use of intrusive surveillance methods?

MELLISH: Yes sir.

LAWSON: You knew that David Norris' father was Clifford Norris, wanted for a large-scale drug importation and that his presence in South-East London could have a significant intimidatory effect, both on witnesses and sources of information, including any supergrass, and that it would be profitable to bring about his arrest?

MELLISH: Yes, sir.

LAWSON: You seemed to arrest him quite quickly.

MELLISH: There was a point where David's birthday was coming up and we hoped that old man Norris would come and visit the boy. We searched the dustbin of David Norris and his mother received a birthday card from the husband which was our first indication that he was in the country and was in communication.

We did surveillance on mum and the boy and we were very lucky. She went down into the country and visited some oast house cottages near Battle, Sussex. We carried on observations and Norris went for a drink. My sergeant got in the pub and gave me a positive ID: it was Norris. I sought permission for an armed operation. The next morning Norris stopped for breakfast at the local café and was arrested.

LAWSON: Thank you. That came about thanks to a combination of surveillance operation, looking in a dustbin and a bit of luck?

MELLISH: Yes, sir.

LAWSON: Your report refers to loaded firearms, handguns, a sawn-off shotgun, and another weapon, an Uzi?

MELLISH: An Uzi machine gun.

LAWSON: And a large amount of ammunition?

MELLISH: Yes, sir.

LAWSON: I will move on, if I may. Intrusive surveillance – that included inserting the video-audio probe into the flat occupied by Dobson? The probe was inserted, in effect making a film?

MELLISH: Yes, sir.

LAWSON: Of what Dobson and his mates, including some of the other suspects, including some Acourts, were saying amongst themselves and doing in the flat?

MELLISH: Yes.

LAWSON: You have described an edited product of that probe revealing amongst that group of young men "a propensity for violence and the carriage of knives and raving bigotry"?

MELLISH: Yes sir.

MANSFIELD: Can I go to MET00510149, it is also PCA00450286. There it is.

The first thing that we see is that, despite Dobson's denials in interviews, he plainly is associating with the very people, one of whom he denied knowing, namely David Norris?

MELLISH: Yes, sir.

MANSFIELD: The purpose of the exercise was to produce evidence against the suspects of motive?

MELLISH: Yes, sir.

MANSFIELD: And that it did in abundance, did it not?

MELLISH: On racism, yes sir.

MANSFIELD: Can I extend it. It is beyond racism. It is racism conjoined with an obsession to extreme violence?

MELLISH: I would agree with that. I think I would add to that, "with knives".

MANSFIELD: There are vast tracks when often Neil Acourt is toying with knives of the very kind that it is thought by the pathologist inflicted the injuries on Stephen?

MELLISH: That is correct, sir.

MANSFIELD: There is another feature – the toying with knives. We can see before they leave through a door in the rear, they will go to the window sill, pick up the knife and they will put it in the inside of their trousers so it cannot be seen whilst they are walking along?

MELLISH: Yes.

MANSFIELD: In addition to all of that, Neil Acourt can be seen on more than one occasion actually demonstrating what I am going to call the modus operandi of this particular stabbing in the Lawrence case.

There are some racially obscene comments throughout the whole of this recording but perhaps the high water mark is when Neil Acourt is heard to say words to the effect: "I reckon that every nigger should be chopped up, mate, and they should be left with nothing but fucking stumps."

Then later David Norris indicates he would like to "go down Catford and places like that with two sub-machine guns and I am telling you, I'd take one of them, skin the black cunt alive, torture him, set him alight." In relation to comments like that by all of the four suspects, is it right to say consideration was given to prosecuting these men for incitement to racial hatred?

MELLISH: Yes, sir.

MANSFIELD: It is the Public Order Act 1986, section 18 (2). May I just read it so that it is clear to the public why no action has been taken. "An offence under this section may be committed in a public or a private place, except that no offence is committed where the words... are used...by a person inside a dwelling and are not heard or seen except by other persons in that or another dwelling."

That was seen to be providing a real practical problem in bringing a prosecution based on this recording?

MELLISH: That is true, sir.

MANSFIELD: Can I just ask, the officer we are calling XX. This is becoming like a Pinter play with surreal references. There is an officer named there in relation to Clifford Norris.

MELLISH: I am pretty sure he was on the Flying Squad at Tower Bridge with me when I was in charge. I was aware that XX had met a criminal in bad circumstances and was disciplined.

MANSFIELD: Neil Acourt was extremely conscious of the fact that something had happened in his room. There is a lot of concentrated interest on the plug and socket and that they are being recorded in the socket. Somebody has tipped them off?

MELLISH: I don't think so. The people at my end were people of utter integrity. There is another possibility which has always been my thoughts on the subject of how and why they suspected from the very first day, if I may give it to you.

MANSFIELD: Yes?

MELLISH: A day or so after the murder, David Norris is involved in it and gets hold of his father. The father sits the boys down wherever, somewhere in London, somewhere out of London, and gives them a very firm lesson in why they must keep their mouths shut, which they have done ever since.

Gives them a very firm lesson in methods of interception.

MANSFIELD: Right?

MELLISH: On technical and telephone. These eighteen-year-old spotty thugs were using the telephone box in the public street and not their own telephone. They had to be briefed by somebody, that is my point.

MANSFIELD: In relation to the Old Bailey trial, the private prosecution, had you known that XX had, in fact, been consorting with the father of one of the suspects – that is Clifford Norris – presumably you would have thought it quite improper, unwise, undesirable, whatever term you may use for him, that that is XX, to have anything to do with protecting, helping, or guarding the main eye witness, victim, Duwayne Brooks, in this case?

MELLISH: What you say is correct.

From the evidence of Ian Johnston, Assistant Commissioner of the Metropolitan Police, 17 June 1998

JOHNSTON: Ian Johnston, Assistant Commissioner, Metropolitan Police, sir.

LAWSON: Mr Gompertz informs me that you wish, on behalf of the Metropolitan Police, to make a statement.

JOHNSTON: Mr Lawrence, I wanted to say to you that I am truly sorry that we have let you down. It has been a tragedy for you, you have lost a son, and not seen his killers brought to justice. It has been a tragedy for the Metropolitan Police, who have lost the confidence of a significant section of the community for the way we have handled the case.

I can understand and explain some of what went wrong. I cannot and do not seek to justify it. We are determined to learn lessons from this. A great deal has changed and yet will change. We have tried over the last four years since the first investigation to show imagination and determination to prosecute Stephen's killers.

I am very, very sorry and very, very sad that we have let you down. Looking back now, I can see clearly that we could have and we should have done better. I deeply regret that we have not put his killers away. On behalf of myself, the Commissioner – who specifically asked me to associate himself with these words – and the whole of the Metropolitan Police, I offer my sincere and deep apologies to you. I do hope that one day you will be able to forgive us.

Finally, I would like to add my own personal apologies for supporting the earlier investigation in ways in which it has now been shown that I was wrong. I hope the reasons for my support will be understood, and I hope that, eventually, you will forgive me for that as well, Mr Lawrence.

LAWSON: You know it has long been suggested by the Lawrence family and by others that the investigation was tainted by racism? What, if any, views do you wish to express about that?

JOHNSTON: It is my firm view that is not the case.

LAWSON: Mr Johnston, soon after you became involved, in the spring of 1994, as far as you were aware, the Barker report was a competent report?

JOHNSTON: I certainly believed it to be so at the time. I accept that it has been totally discredited.

LAWSON: Thank you.

MANSFIELD: May I begin by making it very clear on behalf of Mr and Mrs Lawrence that your initial statement today apologising for what has happened is both welcomed and appreciated.

JOHNSTON: The apologies were heartfelt, sir.

MANSFIELD: Can I go back to some other stages. The Barker review. I want to come to a particular document, MET00890004. This is one of the first meetings you had with the family.

JOHNSTON: In fact, how it happened was, I sat down, I had Mr and Mrs Lawrence on either aside and I read through to them the details, it is the opening page, which in essence gave the investigation, quite wrongly, a clean bill of health.

MANSFIELD: The unexpurgated version had not been written down, namely there were observed criticisms, errors, omissions, and shortcomings which had not been written down.

JOHNSTON: I am absolutely appalled by that. It really is totally, utterly unacceptable.

MANSFIELD: When one turns to the aspect of corruption. Corruption may take many forms. It may not necessarily just be the obvious form of money changing hands but collusion in a wider sense, namely, there is an understanding occurring between organised crime and some people who investigate organised crime. You appreciate the risk?

JOHNSTON: There are subtleties around corruption as there are around racism.

MANSFIELD: There is an officer, who we have been calling XX. Do you know who I mean?

JOHNSTON: I think I know who you are talking about.

MANSFIELD: There was a much closer relationship between Clifford Norris and the officer than he was prepared to admit to. Do you follow?

JOHNSTON: Yes.

MANSFIELD: The first tribunal came to the conclusion that he should be dismissed before he appealed, and he was reduced to the rank of Detective Constable. The question really is this. It really is, would you agree, astonishing that he should be an operational police officer in the detective branch dealing with crime in the very area where the Norris family are thought to have an influence. Would you agree with that?

JOHNSTON: On the fact as put to me, I am appalled that this particular individual is still working for the Metropolitan Police.

KAMLISH: Mr Johnston, I am going to ask questions on the issue of race. You are aware of a recent Met report which shows that black people were four times more likely to be stopped and searched in a street as white people?

JOHNSTON: If we look at the people who are likely to be out on the streets, youngsters who are truanting and excluded from schools, who are over-represented in the statistics, it is young black children. If you look at who else is out on the streets, it is the unemployed. If you look at the differential rates of unemployment, black people, for a range of reasons, some of which are understandable, some of which are abhorrent, are unemployed.

If you look at police where police do their stop and search, it is in high crime areas. High crime areas tend to be areas of social deprivation. Who lives in areas of social deprivation? For a range of reasons, coloured people.

From the evidence of Jamie Acourt, 29 June 1998

J. ACOURT: I do solemnly, sincerely and truly declare and affirm that the evidence I shall give shall be the truth, the whole truth and nothing but the truth.

MACPHERSON: Mr Acourt, would you be seated?

LAWSON: Your name is Jamie Acourt, is it not?

J. ACOURT: That's right.

LAWSON: You understand, do you, Mr Acourt, that in common with all other witnesses giving evidence to this inquiry, you enjoy immunity in the sense that you cannot be prosecuted for anything that you admit to or say today?

J. ACOURT: Yes.

LAWSON: You understand, do you, that you cannot, by direction of the High Court, be asked any questions about whether you did or did not participate in Stephen Lawrence's murder?

J. ACOURT: Yes.

LAWSON: You appreciate that you are required to tell the truth?

J. ACOURT: Yep.

LAWSON: Are you willing to assist the inquiry?

J. ACOURT: Yes.

LAWSON: Let me ask you about knives, first of all. When you were arrested by police on the 7th of May 1993 at your home, as you know, a number of weapons were found, were they not?

J. ACOURT: Yes.

LAWSON: They included a tiger lock-knife and a Gurkha-type knife that were found in an upstairs bedroom. You are aware of that?

J. ACOURT: Yes.

LAWSON: Whose were they?

J. ACOURT: It wasn't my bedroom. I'm not sure.

LAWSON: Whose was the sword and scabbard found under the cushions on the sofa downstairs?

J. ACOURT: Those was ornaments, those was in the house.

LAWSON: Ornaments?

J. ACOURT: Yes.

LAWSON: Why under the cushions on the sofa?

J. ACOURT: I have no idea

LAWSON: Any particular reason, or is that where they are usually kept?

J. ACOURT: I have no idea.

LAWSON: Suggestions that you as a group commonly carried knives are completely untrue, are they?

J. ACOURT: Yes.

LAWSON: Can you proffer any suggestion as to why those suggestions might have been made?

J. ACOURT: No idea.

LAWSON: So the allegation of your being knife-carriers is wholly untrue, you tell us?

J. ACOURT: Yes.

LAWSON: What about the allegations of racism, are they wholly untrue?

J. ACOURT: Yes.

LAWSON: What about your brother, Neil, is it true of him?

J. ACOURT: No.

LAWSON: Your friend, Norris?

J. ACOURT: No.

LAWSON: Dobson?

J. ACOURT: No.

LAWSON: Knight?

J. ACOURT: No.

LAWSON: You attended a committal hearing when you were charged with Stephen Lawrence's murder. Did you see a surveillance video made by the police?

J. ACOURT: Yes.

LAWSON: That was peppered with references to racial comments?

J. ACOURT: I can't remember.

LAWSON: Did you remember all the references to niggers, Pakis?

J. ACOURT: No.

LAWSON: Have you ever come across racists?

J. ACOURT: No.

LAWSON: Is that the truth?

J. ACOURT: Yep. Not what I know of.

LAWSON: You know, do you not, that on the 20th of April you were photographed coming out of 102 Bournbrook Road* with a black bin liner containing something?

J. ACOURT: Yes.

LAWSON: What were you taking in the bin liner?

J. ACOURT: Dirty washing.

MACPHERSON: I asked you originally if you were willing to assist the inquiry and you said yes?

J. ACOURT: Yes.

LAWSON: Do you mean that?

J. ACOURT: Yes.

MACPHERSON: Before anyone else asks you questions I want to ask you one or two: you said you were willing to help insofar as you can by speaking the truth.

J. ACOURT: Yes.

MACPHERSON: As to the racism attitudes of yourself and particularly your brother and the others, having seen the surveillance video, you must know that they showed the most terrible racism. Do you not know that?

J. ACOURT: I can't speak on behalf of other people.

MACPHERSON: No. You have seen the film?

J. ACOURT: I have seen it once and it was a long time ago.

MACPHERSON: The only warning that I will therefore give you is this: you have immunity in connection with the matters which have been investigated in the past but if you commit perjury you may be prosecuted, do you realise that?

---

* The Acourts no longer live at this address.

J. ACOURT: I understand that, I understand that.

MANSFIELD: It's the 3rd of December 1994, you're in custody. You're not there, it's 11.30 at night. I am going to ask you about a specific passage, near the beginning of the transcript. By strange, ironic coincidence, football is the topic of the day. Luke Knight complaining about the commentators wanting the Cameroons, "fucking niggers," to win. Your brother says: "Makes you sick, doesn't it?"

Neil Acourt says, whilst picking up a knife from a window ledge in the room and sticking it into the arms of a chair says: "You rubber lipped cunt. I reckon that every nigger should be chopped up, mate, and they should be left with nothing but fucking stumps." Now, Jamie, have you forgotten that?

J. ACOURT: Yes, I have, yeah.

MANSFIELD: Right. Shocked are you? An honest reply, please.

J. ACOURT: I ain't shocked. It is nothing to do with me. I ain't shocked.

MANSFIELD: David Norris is saying: "I'd go down Catford and places like that, I am telling you now, with two sub machine-guns and, I am telling you, I'd take one of them, skin the black cunt alive, torture him, set him alight."

Then a little further down: "I would blow their two legs and arms off and say, and say, 'Go on, you can swim home now'," and he laughs. Neil Acourt, your brother, says: "Just let them squirm like a tit in a barrel." Do you find all this shocking?

J. ACOURT: I have no comment on it.

MANSFIELD: You indicated that you did know Clifford Norris.

J. ACOURT: I met him when he was younger.

MANSFIELD: After your arrest on the 7th of May did you meet him at all?

J. ACOURT: Not what I can remember, no.

MANSFIELD: Well you know David Norris?

J. ACOURT: Yes.

MANSFIELD: Did he say his father was wanted for major crime?

J. ACOURT: No.

MANSFIELD: Mr Norris never tipped you off about what police might do to listen to you, to watch you?

J. ACOURT: No.

MANSFIELD: You do carry knives in public, do you not?

J. ACOURT: No.

MANSFIELD: In January '93 the police stopped you, you were found in public with a folding lock-knife, were you not?

J. ACOURT: I can't remember all the details.

MANSFIELD: Had you forgotten that you possessed a weapon in public?

J. ACOURT: Until you mentioned it, then I remembered.

MANSFIELD: At 102 – that is the address you were at at that time – quite a large number of weapons were found, were they not?

J. ACOURT: They weren't a large number of weapons, no.

MANSFIELD: Were you present when your room was searched?

J. ACOURT: Yeah.

MANSFIELD: It is clear two just ordinary kitchen knives were found in your bedroom? Did you do cooking in your bedroom?

J. ACOURT: Where was they found in the bedroom?

MANSFIELD: One was found behind a television.

J. ACOURT: No, that weren't in my bedroom.

MANSFIELD: It says: "Downstairs bedroom, Jamie Acourt, two knives."

J. ACOURT: Okay.

MANSFIELD: The revolver. That is a very life-like heavy revolver. What ammunition did you use?

J. ACOURT: It was broken, but it had a pump. I've never used it.

MANSFIELD: In an upstairs bedroom, there was a white jacket which had on it what appeared to be blood staining the right sleeve. Do you know anything about the white jacket?

J. ACOURT: No.

MANSFIELD: In the living room, found between the cushions on the settee, was a sword in a scabbard – this sort of length. What was it doing down the cushions of the sofa?

J. ACOURT: I don't know.

MANSFIELD: I would like you to look at this please. (*Green shirt handed to Acourt.*) This was found on a chair in your bedroom. Is that your shirt?

THE COLOUR OF JUSTICE

J. ACOURT: I suppose so.

MANSFIELD: I am going to suggest to you that you carried knives quite regularly and in the spring of 1993 this shirt demonstrates how you carried them. This shirt, do you see, has six cuts in it?

J. ACOURT: Yes, I can see that.

MANSFIELD: Just kindly tell us how those cuts got there?

J. ACOURT: I couldn't tell you; I wouldn't know.

MACPHERSON: You may leave the witness box.

From the evidence of Howard Youngerwood, Crown Prosecutor, 1 July 1998

WEEKES: Mr Youngerwood, your full name is Howard Youngerwood.

YOUNGERWOOD: Howard Alexander Youngerwood.

WEEKES: In 1990 you became a Crown Prosecutor. I want to flag up, if I may, the code for Crown Prosecutors. Two very important paragraphs.

YOUNGERWOOD: These were the core of the code.

WEEKES: "If the case does not pass the evidential test, it must not go ahead, no matter how important or serious it may be.

"If the case does pass the evidential test, the Crown Prosecutors must decide whether a prosecution is needed in the public interest."

YOUNGERWOOD: A code is no better than its contents. However desirable, however much people might want to prosecute, if on your assessment and in all conscience and under analysis there is insufficient evidence that you simply stop there, whatever private thoughts you might have and however much you want to proceed.

WEEKES: Speak a bit slower?

YOUNGERWOOD: I am sorry.

WEEKES: Can I move on to the Stephen Lawrence inquiry itself. You undoubtedly had the assistance of other Crown Prosecutors who worked on this case.

YOUNGERWOOD: Yes.

WEEKES: We know that the discontinuance notice was dated the 29th of July 1993?

YOUNGERWOOD: Yes.

WEEKES: I would like to know how it came about, the actual notice itself.

YOUNGERWOOD: I became aware roughly at the end of June 1993 that Mr Grant Whyte and Mr Medwynter, between them, were acutely concerned about the state of the evidence.

These were difficult, chaotic days. I sensed that there was perhaps an understandable fear to take a decision they thought was inevitable and they wanted me, quite properly, to take that decision. A fear because of the understandable public concern and apprehended backlash which was entirely understandable.

WEEKES: Right. What happened?

YOUNGERWOOD: My first contemporaneous note made very unhappy reading. Unhappy in both a professional and human being sense. The evidence in my view was even worse than I had been led to believe.

The issue was simply this: the issue was not, was this a racial murder? Anyone who deludes themselves that it was not is not living in this land. But the legal issue basically is the difficult one of identification of a wicked racial murder.

The only identifying witness at that stage was Mr Duwayne Brooks.

The point was that Duwayne Brooks was not identifying the stabber. He had no reason to witness anything that the suspects had done, except they were in a group. Of course he had seen a group. He had described them as young, white men in jeans, but when I was looking at the vital question of identification, the important thing, especially when you compare it with what the other witnesses are saying, is did Mr Brooks see anything of relevance? When you take Mr Brooks' evidence *in toto*, apart from seeing a group converging on Stephen, he had not seen – I do not blame him for this – he had not seen any other battery, physical assault.

WEEKES: Right, we move on to the second point, which is corroboration. What did you understand that to be?

YOUNGERWOOD: There were one or two other witnesses who could have given valuable evidence about a group attack, but on the key difficult issue of identification, we had only one witness, Mr Brooks.

WEEKES: Thank you, Mr Youngerwood.

WOODLEY: I ask questions on behalf of the Senior Investigating Officers in the first investigation. What was your attitude when you heard that the Lawrence family solicitors were planning to launch a private prosecution?

YOUNGERWOOD: I was very, very worried. The evidence was, and I know it causes problems, the evidence was, I can't repeat it enough, sadly, hopeless at that stage.

I was telling Mr Khan I was not behaving like a faceless, boring official.

I was trying to speak to him as a human being who had suffered from racism. It scars my personality. When Mr Khan announced they were going ahead with a private prosecution, I was so desperate, I collapsed in the street. I was ill at home. I had to be physically helped into the office by my wife.

I conveyed increasingly desperately my views, to try and stop this prosecution going ahead, not for improper motives but because I feared what would happen, that we would never get justice.

Blackout.

Closing statement by Macpherson of Cluny

MACPHERSON: Thank you very much. Ladies and Gentlemen, that concludes the evidence which will be heard by this public inquiry in connection with the matters arising from the death of Stephen Lawrence. I should indicate, however, that the future holds much activity and much work still to be done.

Finally, it seems to me right that we should end as we started with a minute of silence to remember Stephen Lawrence and to couple with that our congratulations, if that is the right word, on the courage of his parents.

Would you stand with me for a minute's silence.

A minute's silence.

Thank you very much for your attendance today.

The End.